The Coming Battle
of Germany

The Coming Battle
of Germany

WILLIAM B. ZIFF

WITH AN INTRODUCTION BY
BRIGADIER GENERAL WILLIAM E. GILLMORE
(RETIRED)

DUELL, SLOAN AND PEARCE
NEW YORK

"*Pour les vaincre, Messieurs, il faut de l'audace, encore de l'audace, toujours de l'audace.*"—
DANTON in a speech to the Legislative Committee of General Defense, Paris, September 2, 1792.

ACKNOWLEDGMENTS

THE author wishes to thank the editors of *The American Mercury* for permission to reprint certain sections which originally appeared in the magazine; and for permission to use copyrighted and personal material in this book, grateful acknowledgment is made to the following authors, magazines, and publishers:

The Committee for National Morale, for quotations from its publication, *German Psychological Warfare*; Coward-McCann, Inc., for excerpts from *Air Power* by Major Al Williams; Doubleday, Doran and Company, Inc., for excerpts from *War in the Air* by David Garnett and from *Pattern of Conquest* by Joseph C. Harsch; Farrar and Rinehart, Inc., for quotations from *The Impact of War* by Pendleton Herring; *Foreign Affairs*, for quotations from Grover Loening's article, "Ships Over the Sea"; Harcourt, Brace and Company, Inc., for selections from *Germany Prepares for War* by Ewald Banse; Harper and Brothers, for quotations from *Winged Warfare* by General H. H. Arnold and Colonel Ira C. Eaker; William Morrow and Company, Inc., for quotations from *Armies on Wheels* by S. L. A. Marshall; Oxford University Press, for quotations from *The Nature of Modern Warfare* by Captain Cyril Falls; Noel Pemberton-Billing, for extracts from *Defence Against the Night Bomber*; *The Reader's Digest*, for an excerpt from *The Brainpower of Hitler's Army* by Frederic Sondern; The Ryerson Press, for a quotation from *The Army in My Time* by General J. F. C. Fuller.

CONTENTS

INTRODUCTION

BY BRIGADIER GENERAL WILLIAM E. GILLMORE
U. S. ARMY AIR CORPS (Retired)

WILLIAM B. ZIFF, noted civilian authority on aviation, has at last put down for the permanent and public record the things he has been telling the experts, both military and civilian, during all these extraordinary and world-shaking months of World War II. None of the experts will agree one hundred per cent with what Ziff has to say; but at the same time I doubt that any reader, expert or layman, Army, Navy or Marine officer or average reader of the daily headlines, will be able to put this book aside once he starts reading it. It is dynamite, and by that I mean that it is dynamite of the kind that is needed to win this war.

Not long ago the author of this book made an intensive three-month tour of England. In connection with his writings he was able to visit the airfields, interview personnel and command officers, and among other things discuss highly technical problems pertaining to the broad strategy of the war in the air that will lead, as he hopes, to winning the coming battle of Continents.

But Ziff is not a new man in aviation. Those who have followed his career from the days of the last

World War know that he comes by his interest in and knowledge of aeronautics honestly. He has through all the intervening years been an interpreter of aeronautical matters and affiliated developments. He was editor of the famous old *Aeronautics Magazine* in which the late Brigadier General "Billy" Mitchell made some of his most flaming statements. As editor and publisher of the authoritative aviation journal *Flying*, of *Radio News* and other powerful technical publications, Ziff has earned respect as a shrewd and thoughtful observer of the art of modern war.

Although it was brought up to date at the last minute this book was completely written and ready for the printer before the R.A.F. carried out its terrific bombardments of the German cities of Rostock, Essen and Cologne. The entire technic of these bombardments was outlined in detail by Ziff long before they were undertaken in fact. Months before Pearl Harbor, when abroad, he spoke to America by transatlantic radio advocating this course. Several months before the massive raids on Cologne he wrote his now famous article for the *American Mercury*, projecting the entire strategy of inter-continental air attack which has been elaborated in these pages.

This book projects on a clear-cut screen a picture of the entire new strategy of inter-continental air attack. It is done with solid fact and logic. Seversky, in his *Victory Through Air Power*, posted one theory and part of the doctrine, but this book fills in the blanks. Ziff backs up his statements with an apparently incontrovertible marshaling of "reasons why" and then the "how's" in complete detail.

The "reasons why" are sober, gloomy, almost terrifying. The author shows how we can lose the war not at some future date but *now* by not taking the proper strategic steps and by not utilizing swiftly and correctly the means we already have on hand.

Of late there has scarcely been a day when the sense of Ziff's argument has not been underwritten by bombs dropped by American flyers over Midway, the Aleutians, the Black Sea, the Mediterranean, the Arefura Sea, the Timor Sea, the Coral Sea, and scores of other places around the globe. It is to be hoped that by the time this book is released for publication, its arguments will be even further enhanced by joint American-R.A.F. mass raids on the continent of Europe.

Whatever criticism may be launched at this volume, it is nevertheless one of the most vitally important books ever published in wartime. It makes notably clear the fact that it is not simply production or "weight" of production that will win this war, but a carefully calculated strategy based on our technical resources and geographical position.

If the warning note in Ziff's pages is not heeded, there is a considerable chance that we will be talking about *the coming battle of America* rather than the coming battle of Germany, and Ziff knowing this as well as any man can know it, does not soften his words in his attempt to wake up other Americans. The labors of Ziff and other tireless workers are beginning to bear fruit, and our true position and opportunities are beginning to be completely understood by many of our most influential men in Washington, now so busily engaged in a superhuman effort to expand overnight our war machine.

As any careful reader of the book will soon realize, the various elements auxiliary to our broad strategy are numerous and important. The problems of communication, of transportation, of unifying the command of sea and land and air forces, of organizing production, of providing leadership and sustaining morale, are all dealt with fully and with the kind of stark, compelling, hard-headed realism that distinguishes the book's main thesis. I hope that as many Americans will read this book the day it is published as read, let us say, their local newspaper. If that were to happen, then it seems to me that Ziff would have made a contribution of incalculable importance to our victory.

This book should be read by all members of the Congress. It should help save enormous expenditure of precious American blood and many years of harrowing conflict.

The one final thing I would like to point out is that if my experience is any proof, the reading of this book is going to be anything but a chore to many thousands of others. It is easily one of the most provocative bits of writing on military matters that has been published and made available for a great reading public hungry for an all-American plan for Victory.

Washington, D. C.
June 24, 1942.

FOREWORD

BEFORE Pearl Harbor made it a war of record, no man who dealt in the relationship between cause and effect could doubt for a moment that in all but name the United States had already been at war for a prolonged period.

By every device self-delusion could invent we had pretended that this struggle was none of our affair, that we could avoid it by virtually ignoring its existence, that somehow everything would turn out all right, and that we could cheerfully proceed with the "business as usual" formula, completely protected from the grief and turmoil of the Old World by the two great oceans which roll between.

Suddenly at Pearl Harbor came the realization that our feet had long since been entangled in this clutching web of world conflict, that we had been caught entirely unprepared in a deadly contest which was not the usual war of limited objectives but an out-and-out struggle for the right to exist.

In the orthodox sense the present struggle is not a war such as we have known wars. It is rather a great international explosion revolutionary in its effect on the economics, morals, and politics of man. It has neither boundaries nor limitations. It is aimed not only at our possessions and our freedom, but at all the traditions which make us what we are. It is a dynamic

thrust for all-consuming power by a group of skilled
and insatiable predators experienced in the business of
the kill, who regard us and everything we stand for
with a cold and endless hate.

The only event in history comparable to this ferocious onslaught is the great wave of Mohammedan
attacks on the world ending with the Battle of Tours
in the year 732 A.D. The Arabian warlord, too, was
driven forward by a religion of the sword, by rancorous
hatreds, by a philosophy of blood and iron. Looting
on a grand scale was also an integral part of his system, as was the character of the "divine revelations"
which gave it the frenzy of omniscience. The screaming paranoia of one leader had found its expression in
the *Koran*, just as the latter-day prophet brought forth
the new screed, *Mein Kampf*.

Just as under Hitler and his Nazis, the nihilism of
Mohammed was hungry, savage, and equalitarian.
Every territory which was absorbed contributed to the
ever-growing strength of the advancing legions. They
were under a single, determined leadership, whereas
their opponents were full of dissension and divided
counsels, weakened by luxury and factionalism as well
as by political interference with the military.

It is interesting to note, too, in this deadly parallel-
ism that the Arabs made great use of mobility, fighting a war of infiltration against the slow, heavy armies
of Byzantium and the East.

If we are to have our own Tours by which this new
and seemingly irresistible flood is to be stemmed, we
must recognize the true and dangerous quality of this

struggle. The hour is desperately late and events may be moving faster than we.

Even at this late date few Americans take this war seriously. The view is that we are the best people, that we are the best fighters, and that we have the best production facilities. We will get through somehow; it is impossible for the Germans to beat us, much less the inferior Japs. Our thinking is all in terms of great massings of material and men to be produced on a long-term basis. We plan to bury our enemies beneath an avalanche of weight alone. Until we have produced this formidable force our formula is one of depending on the great blue buffers of ocean for our protection, of playing for time, and of parrying blows. It is based on the belief that the two great seas are our unbreachable Maginot Line, and that we are at least immune to attack on our own continent.

We are engaging in this war without the faintest realization of its true meaning, of the vast cunning, the cold fury, and the enormous armaments pitted against us.

Our attitude is anchored in the colossal misconception which credits to mere physical possessions powers independent of the lean strength and bold hungry courage of men actuated by a shining vision, or by the hard will to victory. It is the philosophy of Philip of Spain and of the great Armada he sent out to conquer the insignificant English, of Darius the Persian who sought to drown the little Greek states in a sea of numbers, of the King Emperors of China who lolled comfortably in their palladia while their vast armies

marched on in a blare of trumpets to smash the up-
start Mongol Genghis who was leading his shaggy
horsemen out of the steppes of Asia.

If we continue to fight the war on these terms we
will finally lose it, succumbing in bewilderment to a
series of iron-hard, surprise blows similar to that of
Pearl Harbor, or to those which destroyed the com-
placent dreams of the French General Staff. The atmosphere in the United States, in fact, is suspiciously
like that which ruled in France previous to the fall of
that once great country.

If we are to win we must make up our minds, first,
in regard to the penalty for losing. The nature of this
penalty was hinted at by Mussolini, when in one of
his theatrical declamations he bellowed to the Italian
people: *"Woe to the vanquished!"*

In this ancient phrase so pregnant with meaning,
the Italian dictator served notice of his recognition
that this was no ordinary war fought according to Mar-
quis of Queensbury rules, in which the loser could
take breath between rounds in order to re-engage in
the struggle again, but a ferocious battle of extermination, a seeking for complete and final mastery.

If we lose, it will end with our institutions smashed
to rubble, as utterly destroyed as were those of classic
Egypt by the fanatic Byzantines, or the empire of
Montezuma by the onrushing Spaniards. Our nation
will cease to exist; its books will be burned, its schol-
ars and savants wiped out, its possessions expropriated,
its men physically enslaved, and its women the play-
things of a conquering horde. Its will to resist will be

systematically crushed; it will be deprived of all possible weapons of retaliation on which an eventual escape to freedom might be based, and as far as the will of man can assure such things, it will be permanently demeaned, degraded, and broken.

If we can once make up our minds that this struggle must be won under any and all conditions of sacrifice, suffering, and pain, then and then only are we prepared to take the necessary steps to make its winning possible. Pure logic drives us relentlessly to the following conclusions:

One: Sitting back on our hind sides waiting for an accumulation of strength can only end in the deterioration of our war effort and our eventual defeat.

We must learn to utilize the matériel, troops, and equipment at our disposal *now* in a continuing, hard-hitting offensive. It is unsound to believe that we can take our time, fighting a delaying action and slowly retreating over the globe while we translate our huge industrial potential into an immense, suffocating force which can win by sheer weight of numbers alone. Much of our wartime production, engines, tanks, and airplanes, is already obsolescent in terms of today's operations. In terms of tomorrow's tasks it will be obsolete. If we are to have the tremendous output of weapons we now contemplate, the loss of the aging equipment now at our disposal should not be disturbing.

Two: We must recognize that the only agencies capable of having any direct effect upon the outcome of this struggle are the Army, Navy, and Air Force.

The intrusion of political officials and civilian bureaus can only affect the conduct of the war adversely, and, to the degree that it exists, directly handicap the activities of the Armed Forces.

We should have a unification of all fighting elements, Army, Navy, and Air Force, under the sole command of some great powerful strategist and tactician, who in turn will be accountable only to the President and the Congress of the United States.

An undisputable unity of command should also exist in reference to the forces of the twenty-eight United Nations. The armed strength and economic power of all should be welded together under a single leadership. The commission form of operation is useless. It fixes neither responsibility nor authority, and is deadly to initiative and enterprise.

Three: We must recognize in their full degree the enormous changes which have been brought about in the science of war by modern industry and invention. The full lethal quality of these new weapons must be given the whole importance due them, irrespective of how much hell this raises with classical notions of strategy and tactics. Organization and strategy outmoded by events of the past three years should be discarded, together with the leaders who insist on adhering to them. New leaders who understand the processes of total war as they relate to a high-powered industrial civilization, and gifted with the imagination to create new techniques out of these giant potentialities, should be put in their places.

Foremost among these latter-day instruments is air

power. Whatever the cost, we must seize and hold command of the air, with special reference to the heaviest bombers it is possible for our aeronautical engineers to build. With these terrible instruments of death in our possession, the full force of the attack should be directed at the very heart of our principal enemies. We should understand that any action which takes place on non-German or non-Japanese territory is indecisive and remains in every real sense of the definition a defensive action. It still leaves intact the mainsprings of the enemy's power and the whole complex of his organized industrial and military strength. No *true offensive action can take place anywhere except directly upon or over the territory of our chief enemy, Germany, or our secondary enemy, Japan.* Our first priority mission is to destroy the Third Reich by a vertical investment of her cities while she is still securely locked in a death struggle on the Russian prairies. Our second is to proceed overland to the shores of the Yellow Sea, rolling up the flanks of the Japanese and then annihilating their islands.

Four: What cannot be attained by an attack in force should be secured by splitting the enemy's morale, by rotting his strength from the inside, systematically sapping his belief in his leaders and the power of his arms, promoting fear, hysteria, bewilderment, and revolution. This great new adjunct to our armed bodies, *psychological warfare*, should be given its proper place in the task force we are creating and should be considered as one of the primary elements in our offensive strength.

Five: We should determine first and last, with unshakeable resolution, never to leave off until we have achieved the unconditional surrender of Germany and Japan. Compromise would be a return to the old calloused wisdom, the cynicism, the every-man-for-himself psychology which characterized the moral decay of the past two decades, and which have all but ended in the disintegration of Western civilization. We must, in particular, guard against the "peace offensives" which will be attempted by Adolf Hitler or those who would replace him. Such a peace could only be an armed truce, with a renewed attack on us as certain as the dawn.

We must take an honest view of ourselves and our purposes. Are we merely a fat, intended victim fearfully struggling against a hungry predator? Or shall we be guided by such a superb detestation of this infamy which has set itself to devour a peaceful world, that we have taken an offensive against it, a sacred oath to exterminate it root and branch? In short, are we simply caught in a corner like some snarling hyena—or are we actuated by a high and youthful dynamism, by grim purpose, by the knowledge of ceaseless struggle against the recurring forces of evil? Only if we are led by that inner light of men who see a duty and a nobility and a beauty in their destiny can we engage ourselves in this struggle and bring it to a speedy and a successful termination. Mere rationalizing will not do it.

Our resolution, strength, and powers will finally be put to the acid test in one of two struggles—the coming Battle of America or the coming Battle of Germany. Either would be the crucial battle of 5000 years of written history.

If we fight the Battle of Germany now, the Battle of America will never be.

The Coming Battle
of Germany

I. INVADE WHERE, HOW?

THE present armed struggle between the United Nations and the Axis powers is the product of violent tensions. These have caused the greatest revolutionary ferment in history. The fate of nations, of religion, of whole races and social structures, is being decided now.

The processes which have given this conflict its revolutionary character have also dictated vast organic changes in the art of war itself. Great as these changes are, they are merely a token of those to come, a warning of the radical revisions in character and constitution of armies and strategy which are impending. The dim outlines of this phenomenon were sensed rather than seen by a number of gifted men of the past generation, by the Englishman Fuller, the Frenchman de Gaulle, the Italian Douhet, and our own "Billy" Mitchell. But even these brilliant visionaries could hardly have been prepared for the fantastic and terrifying shape the war of tomorrow will assume.

Until the advent of World War II the science of war had changed but little. It was essentially a tussle between individual people armed with individual guns, massed together to obtain the greatest possible firepower. Where only armed masses counted in the past, a new factor has now been introduced: the masses are today not in the front lines, but in the industrial machines behind the lines. For purposes of concentrated attack the mechanical monster has taken the place of massed bayonets and cumulatively gained firepower. War has become a matter of output and superior industrial economy. Its efficient operation is vitally dependent on factory facilities and accessibility to raw materials. Only a nation capable of enormous industrial output, manufacturing planes, motor vehicles, guns, and all the other paraphernalia of mechanized war, is capable of military action.

De Gaulle points out, in *The Army of the Future*, that the identical results which great masses of soldiers achieved with difficulty a century ago, are now speedily accomplished by a few perfected machines. A single airplane can do a better reconnaissance job in fifteen minutes than all of Stonewall Jackson's cavalry in a day of reconnoitering. A single .50 caliber machine gun will pump bullets at the rate of 600 per minute, capable of penetrating five-eighths of an inch of armor plate at 500 yards distance and can literally outgun an entire battalion of Civil War vintage. Philippe Barrès describes the conversation he had with his superior officer at military headquarters in mid-May 1940, who lamented: "The entire French army has been disrupted by 5000 enemy tanks and 2000 airplanes to such a point where we are in no position to launch a serious counter-offensive. These German tanks and planes are led and manned by roughly 100,000 troops and opposed to them we have 5,000,-000 practically helpless Frenchmen. . . ."

Not only is there a tremendous increase in massed firepower and the mobility which gives it infinitely greater striking force, but the vast complexity of industrial organization makes all targets infinitely more vulnerable. It is not necessary to claw an opponent apart piecemeal, as in the days of the saber-toothed tiger. If you can strike at his key industrial centers or principal transport and communication systems in sufficient force, your opponent will be mortally wounded. Today a little pellet no bigger than the end of your finger will bring down the biggest animal in the world if you can draw a bead on him and hit him in the right place.

Out of this war is emerging the fact that no nation may seal in its vitals by a wall of protection. The "rear" has virtually ceased to exist and the "front" is wherever an attacking airplane is. Two-dimensional warfare has receded before a new development—that of cubic warfare.

The airplane has already become the principal instrument of battle, of defense as well as attack. It is the single weapon by which control over vast reaches may be established and maintained. While all other instruments of war have more or less reached their peak in efficiency, the airplane is in the very beginning of its development. Under conditions such as those which face the United States today, it is the sole instrument of power, the only instrument that can have any major effect in any decisive theater of operations. The nature of these rapidly emerging realities and the character of the tremendous opportunities they present to us, are far from sufficiently realized. They are hidden in the glare and din of two years of violent military struggle. In this turmoil of kaleidoscopic action, emotion, fact and fancy, it is sometimes difficult to distinguish the forest from the trees, the substantial from the figurative, the stale and obsolescent from the fresh, rugged, and viable. Yet in these lessons of the past the future is written in a mighty projected shadow. It is this we propose to trace.

II

Out of the clear sky, from a commonwealth of cynical pacifists bickering among ourselves over the relative values of various systems of economic and social control, we found ourselves a nation engaged in the grim business of war. Neither intellectually, spiritually, emotionally, nor physically were we prepared.

In our great sluggish attempt to face the rapier-like thrust of an enemy to whom war and conquest are the business of life, we have turned our whole economy upside down. We have disorganized every phase of our national existence. By February of 1942 the authorized total of war expenditures was $145,400,000,-000. Before the year is over they are expected to be stabilized at the figure of $6,000,000,000 a month. These sums may be compared to the total national income for 1941 of $94,500,000,000.

We are making a prodigious effort to remedy the terrible weakness of our situation, and for this purpose we are seeking to throw together great armies. The talk is now of some 8,000,000 men [1] who will be torn

[1] The War Manpower Commission revealed on June 17, 1942, that 6,000,000 or 7,000,000 men will be in the armed forces by the end of 1943, and that this number "eventually" may reach 10,-000,000.

away from whatever useful occupation they may have followed in civilian life and entrained in huge camps, where presumably they will be for the most part drilled and marched, do K.P., and the other routine duties associated with the old concept of mass armies. The raising of this tremendous force represents the clearing out of men by the millions from industrial activities. These men must be fed, trained, and armed. They will consume tremendous quantities of equipment, all of which must be transported. Behind these millions must stand still other millions in civilian life who will provide them with the necessary munitions, housing, and food—and still others who will furnish the raw materials which go into these things.

We have swung on the wide arc of a pendulum. Prior to the war we were not only a non-military nation, but actually a people with a profound contempt for the military. We had a minuscule army of 188,000, equipped with weapons which events of the past two years have proved to be obsolete, and trained along lines which it and its leaders alike must now unlearn.

It seems a fair question to ask: Just how are we going to use this huge pyramiding mass of soldiers? Is it meant primarily for defensive operations, that is to resist an invasion of our own coasts? If this is true, it presupposes that we are going to sit quietly by until the war is brought to us. The experience of the French behind their Maginot Line alone indicates the utter madness of such a policy, and it may be taken for granted that no one would seriously advocate it.

If on the other hand we plan to utilize this vast body of men for a series of offensive operations, a whole host of new problems instantly arises. They must be transported together with all the matériel, equipment, food, and medicines they will require. This brings up the question of ship-bottoms which we do not have, as well as the existence of a safe supply line which we certainly do not possess.

If this is indeed the strategy under which we plan operations, it will mean a long-term period until we can train and equip these men, build the ships to carry them and their supplies, the planes to protect the ships, and the vast organized flow of matériel and men required to sustain and reinforce such an offensive once it has been entered upon.

The protection of this slow-moving armada as it creeps across the bosom of the sea, would naturally fall to our already overworked Navy, a fact which would involve the abandonment of the present convoy system in the North Atlantic leading to Britain, and those which are responsible for deliveries via the Pacific and Indian Oceans to China and Russia. Without considering food, clothing, oil, repair, and replacement parts, an infantry division of 15,000 men is capable of expending over 3000 tons of munitions in a single week of hard fighting. It is estimated that to maintain half a million men would necessitate the constant use of 5,500,000 tons of shipping. Eliminating the tonnage of the accompanying Naval escort, it would require approximately five tons of cargo space to maintain one soldier in the field for a month of active duty.

The transportation system on which any planned offensive must rest is critical. German submarines have increased in the Atlantic by over six times in one year. By the end of 1941 the Nazis had managed to sink some 8,300,000 gross tons of merchant shipping.[2] By the summer of 1942 the rate of loss by sinkings continued to increase materially. What little shipbuilding the British are able to do in the face of continuous bombing, must go to replace their own serious losses, so that the tight little isle can continue to import the foodstuffs, medicines, munitions, and raw materials essential to its continued resistance. The American shipbuilding program, optimistically placed at figures well above 10,000,000 gross tons for 1943, can be hardly expected this year to equal the rate of loss by sinkings.

Despite the governing realities we are being urged by a rising tide of public opinion, as well as by the demands of our fighting ally, Russia, into an unlimited offensive. It is demanded that we send tanks, planes, and men to Australia, to Africa, to various points in Europe—to, in short, carry the war to the enemy by a great land offensive. If this means the transportation of great land armies to the arenas of action, it means fighting the war on the enemy's own terms, since by virtue of his complete superiority of position, numbers, organization, and communications, he may be reliably expected to smash us in detail in every department before we can even get under way.

The British, who have been fighting piecemeal land battles all over the world, have taken a disastrous beating wherever they have attempted a land operation in

[2] Annual Report of the Chamber of Shipping of the United Kingdom (1941).

force. Whether this was in Norway, Singapore, or Greece, they always found themselves in an identical position, outmaneuvered, outgunned, outnumbered, and always without the one element absolutely essential for success—adequate protection in the skies.

Fighting a modern war is largely a matter of logistics. It is governed heavily by the automatic mechanical factor. If, therefore, we are thinking in terms of invading Europe, we must deal with the fact that Germany has approximately 9,000,000 men under arms, of which only a few million are actively engaged on the Eastern front.

It is true that the mere possession of numbers is not in itself decisive. Numbers may be of themselves inert and passive, presenting the need for a qualitative as well as a quantitative measure. The legions of Darius lost to the Greeks, the Chinese to the Mongols; Russia, with a tremendous army, fought three wars with smaller nations, Japan, Germany and Poland, and lost each one. A mere handful of Greeks beat back more than 250,000 Persians at Thermopylae, and at Marathon some 11,000 Greeks ripped 100,000 Asiatic invaders to ribbons. Alexander of Macedon who crossed the Hellespont with no more than 40,000 men, at Issus put to rout the half million men of Darius, and at Arbella won a spectacular victory over what may have been more than 1,000,000 Persians.

Magnificent assaults by smaller forces, as that at Xeres where 12,000 Mohammedans under General Tarik seized Southern Spain by defeating an opposing Christian army of 80,000, depend on ferocity, determination, organization, and mobility. They invariably involve a dynamic force which strikes a stagnant and decaying mass.

Actually the dynamics, organization, and experience may be presumed to be not on our side, but on that of our enemies, whose quality in personnel and equipment may hardly be minimized with safety. It is, in fact, we who would have the immense problem of equipping, training and officering an army which would presumably arrive at its bridgeheads raw, green, untested in actual warfare, the product of a vast improvisation, and beset with huge administrative and organizational problems fully as pertinent to the course of battle as the fighting spirit and the mechanical and motorized equipment these men would use.

They would face a numerous enemy armed to the teeth with every type of weapon modern ingenuity and industry can devise, who would be operating from interior lines, enabling him to strike with stunning rapidity and power against any point of the perimeter from which we might start operations.

The enemy would have, moreover, superb supply lines, whereas we should be obliged to improvise in every respect, with our task force dependent for survival on a line of communications which must be at least described as brittle. He would be near his bases of supply and would have on hand enormous depots of every type of material required in war, great concentrations of oil, metals, textiles, foodstuffs, and other stores we should be compelled to transport. Even more important, he possesses that basic essential to modern war, a "rear" from which he could draw the ground forces needed to attend his war effort; on which he could rely for quick replacement of parts, for repairs, and for that civilian assistance and elbow room which are indispensable to modern military operations.

Our convoy would be under perpetual attack by airplanes, undersea craft, and perhaps surface raiders as well. Granting that this gauntlet could be run successfully under the very noses of hostile guns, there is little reason to believe that a bridgehead can be retained even after it has been achieved. Even presupposing absolute efficiency of organization and operation, neither of which exists today, we must remember that we are starting from scratch. Our military experience in modern terms is practically nil. No comparison may be made with the successful Japanese assault on Malaya and the Indies, since the Japs were able to come in against these semi-barbaric places with overwhelming superiority of ships, men, and planes, literally drowning out the defenders in a towering deluge of armament. In every case their air superiority was gained at once and was never less than twenty to one against the badly armed defenders. This coupled with possession of the initiative made all resistance against them hopeless.

Quite a different situation obtains where an invading fleet enters an area heavily armed and defended by a compact, populous, and industrialized nation skilled in the art of war. If, for example, our primary attack were to be aimed at Italy as has been suggested, from the instant our fleet of troopships entered Italian waters it would be subjected to a continuous and pitiless bombardment from great swarms of killer-planes appearing in such strength as to turn the contest into a slaughter. In back of this savage air fleet would be an Italian army of 3,000,000 men, fighting on its home grounds, and with an expertly organized hinterland from which to draw supplies, reserves, and part replacements. In back of these, in turn, would be the German army sitting like a giant tarantula on the Brenner Pass and ready to strike with dangerous efficiency at a moment's notice.

If Hitler chose he could allow the first contingent of Americans to enter the Mediterranean and even to establish themselves, by simply withholding the huge hailstorm of planes which would otherwise surely be brought against the invaders. When a sufficiently large force of Americans had been caught in this cul-de-sac, he could move down through Spain and close the back door, thus in a single operation cutting off their communications and dooming them to death or surrender. The moral effect of such a disaster would be incalculable, and in this sense might prove decisive.

The opportunities for holding a bridgehead, even on the northern Norway coast, are fully as remote. The British, with complete control of the seas, could not do so after the Germans had once established air bases there. Only one good harbor exists, at Trondheim, which it would be suicidal to attempt to enter. Everywhere roads and railways bristle with guns, and landing fields and airdromes are tied together in a powerfully organized defense plan. Norway today is a tremendous fortress, accessible only to hit and run invaders, and certain to be the graveyard of any army which attempts to land and maintain itself.

The situation in France and Spain is worse, since despite our wishful thinking these Latin governments are dedicated to active collaboration with the Nazi overlords of Europe.

In the Balkans the position is utterly hopeless with Turkey completely unreliable and incapable in any event of holding back the Axis legions for a matter of more than days. The swift smashing of the British Expeditionary Force which had as its allies the brave Jugoslavs and the gallant Greeks, is an augury which cannot be ignored.

No one has seriously suggested that an invasion be made directly upon Germany itself, the single point at which boldness and reckless courage could force a decision. An effort to do so would obviously, under today's conditions, subject to a lunacy commission the military leader who proposed it.

More important than any other single factor which can be brought to bear, the invading American force would lack air protection from the beginning. The range of fighter planes is extremely limited. Our army would have to depend on aircraft carriers, which do not exist at present in sufficient numbers and which are themselves extremely vulnerable to attack. Its heavy bombers would have to come from a great distance and would be without properly prepared landing fields, maintenance and repair facilities, stores of gasoline, and replacement parts. It would be faced with the impossible task of establishing land air bases and achieving a hinterland from which to operate. Facing it would be an unending swarm of ground-based planes massively outweighing the attackers in every phase—in numbers, range, speed, maneuverability, and firepower. Any force which attempted to tie up and make a landing under such conditions would be subjected to such a killing fire that it would be extremely lucky to be able to get back to the comparative safety of the open sea again.

A sober consideration of the problems involved forces the conclusion that until such a time as the military strength of Europe has been sapped by some cause extraneous to the direct process of invasion, German Europe is virtually invasion proof.

Whatever doubts exist in reference to a successful assault upon Europe are vastly amplified when the question of an attack on Japan arises. Here our lines of communication are fantastically long in an area where we do not even have what purports to be naval superiority, and where we are inferior in armed strength of every sort. The best we could hope for would be to attempt painfully to reconquer the East Indies and Southeastern Asia, one chunk at a time, as a prelude to an incursion against the Japanese islands themselves. These places may be assumed to be bristling with arms and fighter planes operating from elaborately prepared bases.

III

The United Nations have entertained all sorts of useless propositions in relation to this war, all of them based on wish-fulfillment and adherence to ideas which run counter to the realities. One of these was the blockade which was not only a failure, but is now rapidly evolving into a counter-blockade, depriving us of essential materials desperately needed for our own war effort. We find ourselves critically short of silk, rubber, and tin. There are serious shortages in aluminum, magnesium, chromium, copper, tungsten, and zinc. We will require some twice as much toluene (basic element in TNT) if our big bombs are to depend on the latter product. Our supplies of nickel, of iron and steel scrap, and chlorine are wholly inadequate. The Japanese conquest cut us off from the great bulk sources of cod liver oil, of which the U.S.A. consumes some 7,000,000 gallons annually, and from practically all of our quinine and rubber.

Much of this will be compensated for by the development of native resources, by substitutes or synthetic products, but these things are the result of protracted evolution, painstaking experimentation and synthesis. They consume time.

The fact of the matter, and one which must be faced, is that we are rapidly becoming a have-not nation. This is one of the factors which must determine our military policy, which will force us to channel our energies in precision planning, in a type of strategy which exacts the utmost advantage from our peculiar geographical position as well as from our remarkable industrial talents and facilities.

The dullest mind by this time rejects the plan that we sit quietly waiting for the war to be brought to us. It is now pretty well recognized all around that the only way to end the war is to take the offensive somewhere, somehow, and to do so with a fury which makes up in aggression what it lacks in opportunity. You cannot kill Japanese and Nazis with blueprints, and you cannot safely seek to make good your shortages in tanks, planes, and artillery by a period of comparative quiet similar to the so-called "phony war" which followed after the collapse of Poland. This erroneous policy enabled Germany to digest what it had and get ready for another powerful blow.

For us any such waiting policy is fatal. While we must build to the limit of our capacity, we are also compelled to strike quickly and vigorously with what we already possess. If we concede the initiative to the enemy, we will find ourselves rapidly pushed backward out of one position after another. Our forces will deteriorate and become apathetic, lacking the will and dynamic power which makes successful attack possible. They will be ruled by the inertia and laxity which always affect idle armies, immobile navies, and grounded air fleets.

Our blows will have to be bold, bloody, and daring—blows in which the opportunities for success have been carefully calculated. Great outlays of money and tremendous accumulations of matériel are not in themselves decisive, whereas the spirit of attack is. This was recognized by thoughtful old Abe Lincoln, who after several years of losses finally said of General McClellan: "He is responsible for the delusion that is untoning the whole army—that the South can be conquered by strategy." [3]

All this was stated with biting brevity by the German military theoretician, Ewald Banse, who asserted

[3] Carl Sandburg, *Abraham Lincoln: The War Years*, Vol. I, p. 554.

that "this test of strength is only apparently a question of armament and preparation—in reality and at the bottom it is a moral affair, in the course of which it must become clear which of the two parties has the stouter heart and the tougher character." [4] In this regard we can learn much from Russia which according to the experts was as good as lost in not more than six to ten weeks after the date of the first German invasion. Everyone believed this but the Russians, and the result now speaks for itself.

Secretary Stimson expressed the national mood when he stated that "we shall seize every opportunity for attack and utilize every opportunity for surprise . . . to do otherwise would be the surest road for defeat." This makes sense. The only thing that doesn't make sense is the means we are utilizing to achieve this end. These consist for the most part of small expeditionary forces which have been dribbling out to all portions of the globe, to Australia, to Eritrea, to Britain, and India. They represent a frittering away of our national resources, no matter how large our army might be. This is made clear by the single fact that Great Britain, which has consistently lost land battles all over the globe, has under arms, including expeditionary forces, troops at home, and various garrisons scattered everywhere, the stupendous figure of 5,336,-943 men. This giant force has been weakened if not thoroughly immobilized by the inherent weakness of the geographical position it occupies, widely scattered, defense and garrison minded, and always compelled to operate on wide exterior lines. Thus automatically

[4] Professor Ewald Banse, *Germany Prepares for War*, p. 61.

it is in the continual process of parrying blows, never being in a physical position to risk all in a great furious campaign which could be decisive.

Despite the claims of those who see in the offensive alone, no matter how rashly undertaken, the open door to victory, we cannot undertake such a measure until pure calculation demonstrates that a concentration of such forces as we control is likely to produce victory. The matter becomes one of mathematics, of comparative likelihoods, of an invoicing of strengths, weaknesses, and probabilities. A well-handled offensive is the result of careful planning, of a deep calculation of the odds which favor the aggressor.

It may not be assumed for a moment that there is some magic in the word *offense* which precludes the possibility of defeat. The great advantage of an offensive is that it allows the attacker to name the time, the place, and the conditions under which the battle is to be fought. But it does not alter any of the basic axioms of generalship. The assailant must still bring to bear overwhelming power at the point of attack. He must be prepared to follow his advantage through with undiminished strength, and all the physical ponderables of the situation should favor his side, whether by virtue of organization and quality or naked brute power. It required only a single miscalculation to throw the legions of Napoleon back from Moscow in utter rout, or fling the Italian Bersaglieri from Greek Epirus in headlong retreat. History is half compounded of offensives which failed, and the record is still far from complete.

II. BLITZ WAR

EVER since the Nazi legions pounded their way to such swift and dramatic victories, a great deal of nonsense has grown up concerning the nature of blitzkrieg and total war. It is assumed that there is some new and utterly irresistible principle involved which may be applied under all conditions. Even military men who remember that Nebuchadnezzar had his chariots and Hannibal his elephants, forget that concentrations of speed and firepower are always relative, that they bear a direct relation to time, space, position, geography, and the fighting strength of the opponent—as well as to that sheer luck which has always blessed the standards of great conquerors.

It is the fashion to see in mechanization—any kind of mechanization—a magic property which automatically dissolves all opposition at a single stroke. The Germans, in particular, have been zealous in propagating this fiction, seeking to identify themselves with the sorcery of inexorable and resistless super-science manipulated by the supermen of this era.

Actually blitzkrieg represents the application of old and classic principles to new methods. It is new only in the complexity of the organization which lies behind it.

There have been conquering states before whose whole business was war, whose luxury was battle, whose ease was looting, rapine, and murder. One of these, the great empire of the Mongols, was the product of a basic strategy strikingly like that of Herr Hitler and his host. It is only with the complex industrial organization which supports the German effort that the identification ceases. Starting as a minor shepherd leader, Genghis Khan reduced and sacked practically all of Asia; and the yak-tails of the golden horde under his lieutenant, Sabutai, were carried westward to the Danube, turning back without ever having tasted defeat.

All the campaigns of the great Khan were prepared by an extensive spy system which combined propaganda among the enemy peoples with an intelligence service entirely alone and superb in its day. Spies operated under the guise of merchants and traders, while threat and terror tactics were an integral part of the entire system. "The greatest joy in the world is to crush your enemies, to see them fall at your feet—to take their horses and their goods and hear the lamentations of their women." Thus spoke the terror of the Eurasian world in the year 1219.

The great Khan always attacked by surprise. The enemy country was entered at several places at the same time. The rapidity of his movements always gave him the superiority of force at the striking point, while tremendous mobility allowed his squadrons to crush the heavy, unwieldy, bewildered armies of Europe and Asia almost at will.

Composed altogether of cavalry (with the exception of a few auxiliary troops),[1] the Mongol advance

[1] Captain B. H. Liddell Hart, *Great Captains Unveiled*, p. 8.

guard was capable of covering as much as sixty miles a day. The enemy invariably found, to his consternation, that the Mongols had turned up in the rear, rendering all communications untenable. The tactics of diversion, of encirclement, were basic to the Khan's scheme of battle. These were conceived and handled in meticulous detail with expert communications maintained by courier and black and white signal flags. Operations were characterized by fine synchronization of movement even between marching columns separated by great distances.[2]

Advancement in the great Khan's army was based on merit alone. His two greatest generals, Chepe and Sabutai, rose to high command before they had reached the age of twenty-five.

Before this terror receded into the twilight of history, almost 20,000,000 people were brutally massacred, whole civilizations were leveled to the ground, and a pall fell over the souls and minds of men which in wide territories of the world has yet to be lifted.

This significant likeness was grasped by Captain Falls, who remarks that total war "is in fact a reversion to the most primitive conception of warfare, the tribal war of extermination which ended in the killing of all the males, the looting of all the beasts, and the burning of all the immovable property of the defeated. It strikes the imagination with new horror only because it is practiced against nations in an extremely high developed state of material civilization." [3]

[2] Brig. General William A. Mitchell, *Outlines of the World's Military History*, pp. 224, 225.
[3] Captain Cyril Falls, *The Nature of Modern Warfare*, p. 5.

The phenomenon we know today as total war has its causality in the huge industrial concentrations born of our technological civilization. The regimentation of materials and men it has made possible; the moral cynicism its failures and inequalities have aroused; the concentration of production, finance, and distribution in a few centers, plus the existence of the gasoline engine, have made the renaissance of total war inevitable.

The army of yesterday was a sort of special caste to which the civilian population possessed no absolute relation. The bearing of arms was a profession and in a certain sense a sport, with a moral code and set of rules all its own, to be recognized by the various contenders involved. Its separation from the political and the industrial was fairly clear. It operated virtually as an independent corporation, and conducted its business by "borrowing" necessary funds from the people and the state in whose name it took the field.

In total war all resources, financial, industrial or human, come under the direct authority of the state and are subject to expropriation or direction without the right of demur on the part of those affected. The state levies on all national assets and conducts its actions against enemy civilians and military alike. All moral deterrents disappear or are rationalized on a wholly utilitarian basis. The object is to capture the opponent's resources intact so that these may be plundered, and every tactic of terror and cruelty which might serve to break the opponent's will is justified in view of the national appetite.

Thus all scruples go by the boards. The attack is undertaken with great secrecy as a lightning maneuver, without any notice or declaration of war. It is preceded by a psychological assault which seeks to demoralize the enemy in advance, destroy his confidence in his leaders and his cause, and to distract his attention from the onslaught soon to be directed against him. Combined with this softening-up process is a carefully engineered subversion, mass espionage, and purchase of innumerable traitors either by funds or carefully gauged emotional appeal. The use of these so-called fifth-column elements is designed to speed the quick break-up of the enemy from within soon after the first impact of physical shock, so as to facilitate the swift control of his population and resources.

Every element of the attacker's economy is brought to bear in the effort to disintegrate organized resistance to his arms. The military forces become the centers of a vast machine in which the producing and distributing elements are the supporting flanks.

The Germans, who developed the technique of blitz in association with the master strategy of total war, learned these tactics from five men, none of whom was German and each of whom was a prophet without honor in his own country. One was Gustave Le Bon, French master of mass psychology whom his own compatriots practically ignored. Others were the great Englishman, J. F. C. Fuller, whom his own contemporaries looked on as a crackpot, and the gaunt Frenchman de Gaulle, both champions of the renovated war of movement. They preached that great concentrations of tanks moving as the spearhead for a limited professional army which followed close behind on wheels, would create such irresistible points of pressure that the existing type of fortified lines would simply fold up under it.

The other members of this fistful of brilliant thinkers were the Italian, General Douhet, and the American, General Mitchell, who claimed that the decisive factor in modern war would be the tremendous striking power of the airplane. Mitchell's freely-spoken contempt for those who resisted his views, afterwards proven correct, caused him to be court-martialed, while Douhet actually spent a short period in jail.

The Germans co-ordinated all these factors with other elements of their vast army to create what has since become known as *the fighting team.* This involves perfect synchronization between all branches of the armed services, under the direction of a quick-acting, hard-hitting, responsible leadership, a development of initiative which reaches into all ranks.

The single factor which dominates the structure of such an armed body, and hence the nature of the strategy open to it, is the existence of the gasoline engine together with the network of paved highways which has followed in its train. These arteries all lead directly to the enemy's heart, to his manufacturing, political, and storage centers, to the switchboard from which all his operations are controlled. These conditions, fully ripened, were responsible for the abandonment of the war of fixed position. Modern warfare becomes largely one of roadways and swift movements, surprise attacks and tremendous concentrations of forces which suddenly appear seemingly out of nowhere.

Co-ordinated with these actions, as an essential part of the fighter team, is the light bomber, turned now into a screaming, deadly, plummeting artillery platform supplying the single great need which could make blitz war successful. The principal function of the dive-bomber is that of demoralizing the artillery defense of the enemy which otherwise would blast the advancing tanks off the map.

At the same time the air force attacks vital points behind the line, munitions dumps, communication centers, power stations, bridges, and aqueducts. Hedge-hopping airplanes blast the troop masses which are being brought up to the front, in an effort to further demoralize the roads. The "front" as a rigidly existing factor tends to disappear, and once the break-through has been accomplished, becomes extremely fluid so that it may be said to exist universally and not locally.

Parachutists and air-borne infantry, dropped at strategic points, add to the whole melee of disintegration. The entire system places an enormous premium on ingenuity, daring, co-ordination and rapidity of action, throwing the enemy into utter confusion and allowing him no opportunity to bring up reserves to close the gaps in his line. Perfect timing is an essential factor. Everything must come off exactly on schedule. Otherwise the maneuver becomes a mad one with the long, thin attack column deployed over the road, ready to be chopped off by a determined counter-attack.

The attack also suffers from the weakness of being self-liquidating, since under normal conditions artil-

lery and automatic weapons of all kinds concealed in
natural cover along the road, would blow the attacker
into Kingdom Come and pile up an accumulation of
debris which would make movement virtually impossible. It is here that the dive-bomber takes on a decisive role by acting as the cutting edge of the advance, clearing its path and knocking out artillery and
automatic gun emplacements which might otherwise
have made the total maneuver a hopeless adventure
from the beginning.[4]

Since by its very nature a modern mechanized army
is capable of swift concentration at almost any given
point, the element of surprise is overwhelmingly in
favor of the attacker, who can also, due to this factor
of mobility, make almost instant use of the production facilities of the conquered country, thus in a
sense living off the land. He can bring up his men
and matériel to any place, along roads which make a
speed of eighty miles a day not unusual.

Such a war becomes a series of attacks in unceasing
waves. Its object is to keep the enemy continually on
the defensive, to feint and threaten in every direction
at the same time, until a weak point is found in the
opposing defense structure. There is then a swift mass-

[4] Brig. General Ira Eaker and Lieut. General H. H. Arnold point
out in *Winged Warfare* that one decisive battle was fought in the
first World War which presaged the success of future dive-bombers,
and which military men generally overlook—the campaign of Al-
lenby in Palestine, where a Turkish Army of more than 100,000
men was cut to pieces by the use of attack aviation. This was known
to military leaders of all the world for two decades prior to 1939,
"yet apparently it stirred nobody but the Germans to a full realization that a new concept for employment of airplanes had come to
land warfare."

ing of forces at this point with an attempt at a rapid break-through, capture of the enemy's vital areas, destruction of his communications, and the encirclement of that portion of his armies which have been cut off, so that they may be further bisected and destroyed at leisure.

A classic example in which each of these factors was apparent was the break-through in the Ardennes Forest. Twice the Germans massed their armies opposite Holland and Belgium in the North in gigantic feinting operations, to determine what the Allied leaders would do. Each time the English and French moved their armies into the gap to receive the shock of the expected attack. The third great feint on the part of the Germans saw Gamelin and Gort again wheel into Belgium. This time the Germans threw tremendous power into an assault on a supposedly impregnable sector, weakly defended by poorly trained reserves, the Ardennes Forest. From this massive break-through and its aftermath, which sealed the fate of all stationary defense lines, the Allies never recovered.[5]

Variations of this technique were introduced to meet the needs of each peculiar situation. In Poland dive-

[5] Each time Gamelin pushed forward into the expected breach, he exposed his own defense lines and laid himself open to a smashing blow toward his rear in the unprotected plains of Flanders and Champagne. It took the Germans less than forty-eight hours to crack through and cut across the Meuse, severing the Dutch from their Allies and outflanking the latter's supply lines. The break-through itself followed strictly according to plan—heavy tanks preceded by dive-bombers and followed by the engineers and motorized infantry. With open country ahead of them, the panzer units moved swiftly ahead, crushing the Belgians and French in a nutcracker maneuver.

bombing was combined with low level attack [6] to blot out Polish aircraft before they could take to the skies; to put airdromes, bases, railroad centers and other forms of communication out of existence, so as actually to prevent the mobilization of the Polish Army itself. Within a few days the Polish Air Force was destroyed, train and telephone service collapsed, and the Polish Army degenerated in consequence into a number of guerrilla forces practically out of contact with each other.

In Holland the Germans opened their attack again with aircraft attempting to destroy Dutch planes on the ground. As soon as the bombing ceased large transport planes, protected by fleets of Messerschmitt Me-110's, appeared, dropping great numbers of paratroopers. These were dressed in Dutch and British uniforms to add to the general confusion, and with the aid of native traitors, were quickly able to surround and capture a number of strategic stations. This type of attack from the rear played a decisive function in demoralizing not only the physical but moral resistance of the enemy, who found his normal dispositions in a pandemonium of disarrangement.

In Belgium and France these tactics were varied by the use of agents who spread the wildest rumors behind the lines, and by aerial attacks on civilian popu-

[6] A type of assault in which a flying artillery platform, moving at 300 to 400 miles an hour, comes in following the contour of the ground, at a height of some seventy feet. The unusual angle of attack combines high firepower with tremendous surprise. The attacker delivers his message of death almost at the moment he is seen. Low flight prevents the use of the anti-aircraft artillery commonly utilized against airplanes, and also makes it difficult to track the plane with machine-gun fire.

lations, who were machine-gunned and stimulated to flee to the roads, thus clogging them hopelessly and impeding their use by the defending forces.

II

Whatever lessons we are to learn from the easy victories of the German *Wehrmacht* should be gained by cautious examination and analogy, rather than by slavish imitation. Much of it will be found not to apply to our own particular tactical situation at all.

The amazing success which attended these lightning German maneuvers has given us an entirely false conception of the conditions which produced them and made them so extravagantly effective. If we seek to build an army modeled directly upon the German experience in Europe we will be building one which can have no conceivable relationship to any strategy open to us. This, and not the example of stupendous German successes on the Continent, is the lesson we must learn from two and a half years of bitterly waged blitz war.

No responsible military man in Europe had been prepared for this type of operation. On the very eve of World War II the German expert, Rosinski, makes it perfectly clear that the great body of German military leaders rejected the principles of *lightning war* "such as has been drawn recently in certain sensational publications." These ideas, Rosinski complains, "represent the views of the Nazi party and of its adherents within the circle of the high commanders." It is by no means certain, he continues plaintively, "that the sober professional opinion of the majority of the commanders and of the general staff will prevail against the fantastic vagaries of Nazi amateur strategy." [7]

The French still clung to the classic method of utilizing tanks, tying them down to the slow pace of the advancing infantry, thus depriving them of their principal asset, speed, and of the shock tactics this made possible. The Germans, who had only a small number of panzer divisions, regarded them as a weapon of opportunism which could not always be certain to find the special conditions they required to be effective, and were themselves startled by the terrific hitting power of this arm in actual practice. In France de Gaulle, and in England the brilliant General J. F. C. Fuller,[8] who were looked on as fanatics and extremists, had their counterpart in the German, General Heinz Guderian, whose view was expressed in the dictum: "Where tanks are, is the front."

The dynastic authority of the land battleship, or even of the fighter team, has by no means been assured despite the startling series of military events set in motion by the Germans since the fall of 1939. The Nazis were simply the first to demonstrate the power of the tank by utilizing it as an independent arm. The decisive nature of their triumphs is no more convincing when applied to all conditions, than the tremen-

[7] Dr. Herbert Rosinski, *The German Army.*

[8] Fuller's remarkable book on the nature of mechanized warfare, which stands on a par with de Gaulle's astonishing work, was not read by Englishmen, who practically ignored it, as did the Americans "though 30,000 copies were published for the German army and the work was also widely circulated through the military forces of the U.S.S.R."—S. L. A. Marshall, *Armies on Wheels,* p. 17.

dous victories of the armored horsemen of Cortez against the vast multitudes of Montezuma, or of the greatly outnumbered English archers whose long bows smashed the ponderous age of chivalry, together with the mailed knighthood of Europe, at Crécy.

The advent of the fighter team is an important fact in military history, but certainly not one whose application would be decisive universally. It ranks with the revolutionary use of gunpowder to reduce the supposedly impregnable city of Constantinople in 1453; or with Napoleon's sweeping revisions in the handling of field artillery, which dominated a century of European war-making.

We are apt to forget that it is the element of consternation induced by newness which may be as great a part of the effectiveness of some recently introduced instrument of battle as any other. A comparable situation was the rise of the *General Staff* coincident with such radical developments as the railway, telephone, and telegraph. Studied campaigns of action, prepared in scrupulous detail, took the place of inspirational decisions by great field commanders. At the battle of Königgrätz the precise planning made possible by superior communication and transport systems, introduced the omnipotent General Staff scheme. Based on these then fabulous methods, the obscure Prussian, von Moltke, sealed the fate of the whole campaign in six days of brilliant action.

No great introduction of strategy or arms is as effective later as it was at the beginning. Sooner or later forces gather which first neutralize and then defeat it. It is impossible to introduce any new weapon without changing the conditions which relate to it. "Every change in condition," states Marshall, "modifies the application of the principles of war. Each weapon is influenced by ground, time and space, as well as by every other weapon. As new conditions are established these react upon the power of weapons."[9] In North Africa the appearance of a new mobile long-range anti-tank gun completely nullified the strong numerical advantage in tanks held by the British, throwing them back on their heels to their Egyptian bases.[10]

Today it is a habit to think of the tank as invincible, though a generation ago the two great opposing generals, Ludendorff and Haig, considered it unimportant; while until the very outbreak of the present war the French and English General Staffs counted it at best an auxiliary to the all-powerful infantry.

Without absolute air control over the area of attack the entire tank assault collapses. If the defending artillery remains intact, neither panzers nor motor-borne infantry can approach. It was the dive-bomber which removed the panzer's neck from the chopping-block and gave it the "occupying power" which allowed it to move on far ahead of the supporting foot-soldiers. Yet today the dive-bomber itself may be through as a type since it is subject to heavy fire from ground weapons, the only airplane, in fact, which is really vulnerable to ground attack. The British at Dun-

[9] *Armies on Wheels,* p. 158.
[10] Rommel's 88-mm. anti-tank guns were able to knock out the Lend-Lease M-3 Grants, while remaining safely beyond the range of retaliatory fire. This proved a decisive influence in the Libyan struggle.

kerque discovered that if they stood their ground the dive-bomber was a perfect target, whereas opposing soldiers had previously been unnerved by the deadly screeching and ferocious power-dives of these craft.

As time goes on methods of dealing with tank attacks improve, just as methods of dealing with armored men in the past improved and finally outmoded them. More effective anti-tank guns are developed, roads are mined at intersections, individual houses become fortresses in which small anti-tank guns and mortars can be hidden. Aircraft cannon already enable planes to cope with light tanks and soon may be expected to carry heavy enough guns to make tanks of every type as vulnerable as so many cheese boxes.

The progress of the campaign in Russia makes a revision of all blitz war concepts necessary. Although the war still remains one of infiltration, the front as a continuous line has disappeared. It has become, instead, a mobile and elastic belt of territory involving not lines but zones. Its original principles were evolved by Chiang Kai-shek long before they were known in Russia, as a protection against Japanese tanks, artillery, and airplanes. The Chinese employment of this so-called defense in depth is to use belts up to thirty miles wide full of barricades, barbed wire, machine-gun emplacements and other available types of obstacles. Layered in front of and within these barricades are riflemen who are the front area of defense. Far in the rear is such artillery as the defender possesses.

The Russian defense in depth is much more elaborate due to the availability of greater resources, but it is designed on identical principles. It consists of an outpost zone held by a small mobile detachment, then a sector fortified with anti-tank mines, at the back of which are various belts of steel and concrete barriers. These various layers, together with ditches and methodically scattered fortresses, give way finally to the mass of counter-attack troops which lurks behind.

The entire zone may be anywhere from thirty to seventy miles deep, and operates on the principle of a giant shock absorber or self-sealing tire. Whereas the brittle, fortified lines in the West could be breached by simply piercing them, the new defense in depth was designed to close down on all entering bodies, neutralizing the first fury of their impact.

In the beginning, the Russians had probably as many tanks as the Germans, but no organized tank armies. They utilized the tank in much the same way as the artillery, as an auxiliary to marching men. As a result the Muscovites lost much of their tank effectives, a loss from which they still suffer. Reeling backward in a grim battle for existence, the Russians finally rectified this serious error. Their new, hastily-formed armored brigades were designed for even more flexible tactics than those used by the Germans, to take the fullest advantage of the vastness of the Russian terrain. They were a good deal smaller than the Teuton divisions and operated from a multiplicity of small bases or fortified points which acted as pivots for both attack and counter-attack.

Here apparently was a marked improvement over the German style of organization and part of the reason for the startling comeback of the seemingly beaten Muscovite army.

Now it was the Germans who were forced to make an accommodation to a new style of operation. Completely dwarfed in a vast landscape where roads were scarce and no central nerve masses existed whose death could be relied on to put the entire organism out of existence, the Nazis found that the *keil und kessel* tactics so successful in France and Poland simply left formidable Russian armies in their rear.

The Russians, who maintained their communications by wireless and truck over prairie reaches, simply ignored the catechisms which had them automatically beaten, and introduced a new principle—that of an envelopment which operated on several levels, so that the surrounder always runs into some danger of being himself surrounded by his own maneuver. This placed the Germans in the disagreeable situation of proceeding further and further into a feather mattress.

It is not unusual to find important engagements being fought fifteen, twenty or even fifty miles in the enemy's rear or on his flank. It is commonplace, too, to find cavalry conducting successful engagements sixty or more miles behind an enemy held line.

The effect of the wild shrieking *Stuka* was largely lost on the Russians who were not frightened by this hellish apparition. The Muscovites learned to use their own limited aviation in massed waves or in the sense of true air power, only incidentally tied to the ground formations, strafing and bombing the invader's troops, supply lines, and depots. Here, too, was something quite different from the bewildered textualism which had frozen the operations of the Allied high command in the West. Blitzkrieg under these conditions is robbed of most of the surprise element on which it depends and its precipitate speed deteriorates rapidly into exhaustion.

Thus every principle by which blitz war was recognizable in its previous operations on the Continent, has disappeared. Its technique is now in a state of flux in an effort to make an adjustment to a totally alien and baffling set of circumstances. No part of the power of the German *Wehrmacht* has been lost; but its ability to obtain a decision has been dissipated by the fact of the limitless Russian steppes and by the ability of the Russian people to accommodate themselves to the altered face of modern battle.

The result is shown in the German losses in this indecisive campaign, probably totaling some 2,000,000 men. Previously, in all the battles of the Balkans, Poland, and Western Europe German casualties had been less than 100,000 all told.

Just as the single element of Soviet landscape was to have so profound an effect on the course of this war, so another physical factor—that of simple geography, will bear upon and perhaps determine completely its outcome.

The astonishing situation which arose directly from this factor and which could be studied with profit by those who think in terms of mass armies and great physical invasions, is the continued existence of England as a potent resisting force after more than two and a half years of war.

No one may claim that England has an army worthy of consideration in the same breath with the vast German establishment which faces it only twenty-two miles away across the English Channel; and no one will assert that the English had any army at all after the fall of France and for many ensuing months. The home guard amounted to little. And the tattered remnants of the once proud B.E.F. who had managed to return home after the memorable evacuation of Dunkerque, were armed with little more than courage and the will to resist.

Since that time the vast churning *Wehrmacht*, the greatest, most efficient and formidable military establishment in history, has been forced to remain impotent while it watched the Islanders rise from a despised and broken opponent to possession of a sizable army and the most magnificent air force in existence. And the fuming Nazi has seen the shattered English finally, after more than two years of effort, succeed in organizing a worldwide coalition with which to smother the Axis out of existence.

It is the phenomenon which accounted for this fantastic situation which we can study to our advantage, since it also applies to us.

III. THE RISE OF AIR POWER

FACED with these revolutionary changes in military methods, the Englishman, Viscount Gort, and the French Gamelin, touted as the greatest professional soldier of his time, huddled in amazement behind their fixed defenses as they saw the Germans climb like an inexorable wave over obstacles which were thought to represent insuperable barriers to any penetration except at the most terrific costs. General Chauvineau's axiom that the attacker must have three times as many infantry effectives, six times as much artillery, and twelve times as much ammunition if it hopes to dominate the defense, ruled the thinking of the French General Staff. "France," asserted the eminent General Weygand, "is impregnable." The aging Petain, third member of the dominating clique of generals, held that the supreme lesson of World War I was the superiority of fortified positions. He believed "that where fortifications had failed during the war it was through bad design in relation to the dominant conditions." [1] English thinking was best expressed in a smug plan for a war of attrition developed in the pages of the military writer, Liddell Hart.

When early in May 1940 the Germans, who had brushed aside the supposedly impassable obstacle of

[1] Marshall, *Blitzkrieg*, pp. 80-81.

the Low Country fortifications as if they were cobwebs, came thundering into Northern France, indescribable confusion gripped the Democratic allies. They did not even know the disposition of their own armies. They had lost control of the air. They were the victims of a series of hammer-like blows coming suddenly from all directions.

When Leopold of Belgium folded up on his flank it appeared as if the end had come for the British commander, Viscount Gort. Confidently, the English had put all their eggs in this single basket. All British tanks and heavy equipment, their big guns, their great stores of ammunition, not to mention almost the whole of their experienced military staff, lay hemmed in the crook of von Brauchitsch's encircling arm.

Desperately the hopelessly cornered B.E.F. fought its way toward the Channel Coast. The Germans, not realizing the resolution and resources of character which made this little force formidable, leisurely awaited its surrender and pursued the main French armies.

For once the British acted with intelligence and decision. They essayed the bold maneuver of evacuation from Dunkerque, although its successful completion seemed impossible. The story of the many small boats of all types which raced through the French harbor to rescue the English Army is well known, but what is not thoroughly realized is the fact that the British threw into this operation the whole of what remained of their admirable air force. The success of this entire operation was due to the British fighter planes which, against enormous odds, kept command over the air at Dunkerque and the Channel.

In their retreat to the beaches the British had abandoned most of their heavy equipment. They were without artillery and in some cases even without rifles. Their only surface guns were those of the Royal Navy, which held their left flank and put up a heavy anti-aircraft fire.

The German bombers came in escorted by the usual Messerschmitt fighters. They were met by a cloud of British Spitfires, Hurricanes, and Defiants.

The British were handicapped by being forced to operate from bases in England, seriously limiting the ability of the short-ranged fighters to remain in the air over the site of operations. On the other hand they were aided by a providential fog, plus a dense screen of smoke resulting from nearby oil storage tanks which had been set ablaze.

The German air corps, under Grauvert and von Richthofen, swarmed in to sweep the roads of approach, the beaches, and the harbor waters with killing fire. British tactics were compelled to rest on interception. At any and all costs complete mastery of the air had to be established over the points of embarkation and the Channel waters.

The Nazi planes found themselves powerless to break through this wall of interception which British steel and courage erected. During a single 36-hour period 121 German planes were brought down by the completely outnumbered British fighters. During the nine days of the evacuation the British shot down 377 Nazi craft and lost only 87.

In this triumph of air power 325,000 men were saved.[1a] Their rescue provided the British with the nucleus for a new General Staff, and for the officers required to train a new people's army. What is more, it gave them heart and a feverish understanding of the potentialities of the air arm. In a desperate race against time they immediately concentrated their meager resources on it.

Had the German General Staff read correctly the meaning of this local struggle, they could have taken warning. It would have been clear that flushed with success as it was and despite its quantitative superiority, the *Luftwaffe* was totally unequal to the task of reducing Britain itself. In speed, firepower, maneuverability, and in the individual training of fighter pilots, the English were infinitely superior to anything the Germans had in the air. Hereafter, too, the Germans would have to attack from continental bases, drastically cutting down their already short range and staying power.

Dunkerque proved conclusively that even an army hopelessly beaten in the field, disorganized and without adequate weapons, can be rescued if it can maintain local superiority in the air long enough to bring the operation off. Gazing with strange prescience into the crystal ball of fate, Winston Churchill observed: "There was a victory inside this deliverance which should be noted. It was gained by the Royal Air Force."

[1a] This included 123,095 Frenchmen who had fought their way to the beaches alongside of their British comrades.

At this point Hitler himself, completely misjudging the real value of the sequence of events which had ensued, made that mistake tragic to his hopes, which cost him the World. As Hannibal is said to have cried, "O, Cannae! Cannae!" after his neglect to occupy defenseless Rome had rendered the victory of Cannae sterile, Hitler could well weep, "O, France! France!" Instead of swinging all his resources for an immediate crossing of the Channel at whatever cost, allowing the inept French under Weygand to solidify themselves behind a new line of defenses on the Somme, he reverted to classic strategy. He proceeded to pursue and destroy the French Army, leaving the breathless British virtually to themselves. Had he thrown his divisions over in boats and barges under a canopy of planes and preceded by an advance guard of bombers, in an all-out effort, he would have paid a fearful price but his success would seem to have been assured. His ultimate victory over the French was inevitable in any case.

German newsreels show *Der Fuehrer* receiving word of the French request for the armistice. His actions were most extraordinary—he snapped his fingers, kicked his heels, chortled and goose-stepped out to his office. The Nazi leader evidently considered the war over and the world all but won. A few weeks later he received the capitulation of the French in a railroad car at Compiegne and waited confidently for the British to surrender or offer terms. He judged them to be weaponless—which indeed they were, but he neglected to consider the existence of the Royal Air Force as a potent and, as it proved, invincible shield. Twice he offered the British terms which from his own view were actually magnanimous. Disdainfully they were refused. His patience worn to a shred, Hitler finally decided to attack an island whose facilities, particularly for shipbuilding, he would have preferred to take over intact by negotiation.

Now began one of the strangest battles, and one of the most conclusive in its effect, in military annals—the Battle of Britain. As a phenomenon it is comparable to the stand by the little band of Greeks at Thermopylae against the huge waves of invading Persians. On the British side this battle will rank with any in Crécy's list for its decisive effect on the course of history.

II

On July 19, 1940, in a speech to the Reichstag, Hitler had offered what he considered a reasonable peace to the British, suggesting that he would allow them a prominent place in his New Order. He said: "I can see no reason why this war must go on."

When it became clear that Churchill had no intention of accepting this proffer, the German Fuehrer's anger was unrestrained. He shouted in his speech of September 4, sarcastically: "In England they are full of curiosity and keep asking, 'Why doesn't he come?' Be calm. He is coming! He is coming!"

The military position at the moment the German leader uttered this threat was as follows: in supreme command on the Continent, and virtually allied with Soviet Russia—the only possible opponent who might offer the slightest difficulty—flushed with unbelievable success, sat the German armies under von Brauchitsch, Keitel, Guderian, and Milch. It was not only the best organized, the best drilled and the finest equipped military horde in history, but perhaps also the most numerous. The bloody smell of victory dilated its nostrils.

Across the Channel lay the quarry—defeated, disillusioned, unhappy, with neither ordnance, matériel, nor trained manpower. The British Army, as has been stated, practically did not exist as an effective fighting force. The great British Navy was for all useful purposes neutralized and did not dare enter the Channel for fear of a disastrous pounding by Nazi dive-bombers.

The plan was to tow an invading host across the Channel—fitted out with tanks, artillery and other necessary mechanized equipment—on flat scows drawn by small, fast boats. With great sagacity the prudent Nazi high command had provided also for a large number of self-propelled barges. These were gathered in the invasion ports of Holland, Belgium, and Northern France and were of all sizes up to 3000 tons.[2] Heavy guns would be set up on both ends of the French Channel Coast to keep the crossing clear of interference by British ships or ground guns. Overhead the landing was to have been protected by a mighty umbrella of all-powerful fighter planes. No

---

[2] These craft were peculiarly suited to land tanks or armored cars on beaches. They could be run right up into shallow water and on to land by means of ramps. It is estimated that these barges alone had a carrying capacity of 1,000,000 tons, while that of the ships amounted to around 4,000,000. They made a lovely target and the R.A.F. was not slow in taking advantage of the fact.

wonder Reich-Marshal Hermann Goering licked his jowls in anticipation and bellowed, "There are no unconquerable islands any more." [3]

To the German high command this final mopping-up operation, prelude to a swift attack on the United States, was hardly more than a piece of well-calculated routine. Nevertheless, in their methodical way these men realized that the invasion could not come off properly until the little English air force was blasted out of existence. Then Britain would lie entirely at the mercy of this new conqueror who had taken up where Napoleon had left off.

On August 8, the Germans began their assault, commencing with a series of air attacks on coastwise shipping, ports, and airdromes. Secure in their knowledge of tremendous numerical and, they believed, tactical superiority, Goering and Milch sent over great mass formations of bombers. These were escorted by echelons of single and twin engine fighters, Junkers 87's and 88's, Heinkel 111's, and Dornier 17's. Their object was to destroy British fighter craft on the ground, render air bases useless, and clean all hostile shipping out of the Channel—largely a duplication of the measures so successful on the Continent. Ports and communications could then be destroyed without opposition, the military forces of the British paralyzed, and the German armored divisions placed in a position to operate undisturbed.[4] They sought a swift decision

[3] June 2, 1941.
[4] *Battle of Britain*, British Air Ministry Record from August 8 to October 31, 1940, p. 12.

which would end the war in one more great sweep of the German broom.

Facing this invading host was a group of perhaps 1000 British fighters, mostly single-seater Spitfires powered by Rolls-Royce-Merlin engines, and the somewhat slower Hawker-Hurricanes.

Both types were faster and more maneuverable than any of the German models brought up against them.[5] The backbone of the British fighter command was the Spitfire, which de Seversky called "the most effective single-engine fighter in the world." [6] Both Spitfire and Hurricane possessed eight free-firing machine guns installed in the wings, with vulnerable spots well armored. The importance of this single fact in combat may be judged from Sir Archibald Sinclair's [7] remark that "the decision to adopt the eight-gun fighter like the Hurricane and the Spitfire, may well rank as one of the great decisions in the history of the war."

The German fighter planes on the other hand, for all their boasted superiority, were the products of mass output, a fatal flaw in a fluid situation where swiftly-evolving technical improvements could give qualitative supremacy almost overnight. "The Germans got ready for war so early," says Narracott, "that by the time it came, many of their aircraft were obsolescent and some even obsolete." [8] These had been the last word in perfection at the time of the Spanish Civil

---

[5] The Spitfire could probably do then in the neighborhood of 350 miles per hour; the Hurricane around 330.
[6] *Atlantic Monthly*, March 1942.
[7] British Minister for Air.
[8] A. H. Narracott, *How the R.A.F. Works.*

War, but in the competitive, fast-changing conditions of actual combat their palmy days were over.

The best German types were at least fifty miles slower than the British and were not nearly as maneuverable or well armored. More serious still, their firepower was both limited and fixed, developing blind spots of which opposing craft were quick to take advantage.

The same relative differences of superiority applied to the bombers possessed by the two contestants. Due to the influence of General Ernst Udet, the German bombers did not carry heavy defensive armament and relied principally on fighter escorts plus speed. Their load capacity was usually not great due to limited range, and did not average more than one ton. In most instances their combat power was so poor that "they could meet an eight-gun assault from a British pursuit with only one gun, making a hopeless ratio of eight to one." [9]

As a task force, the Luftwaffe proved itself utterly incapable of its mission. This weakness was the direct product of its earlier success on the Continent. Though it was a separate arm co-equal with the German Army and Navy, it possessed none of the qualities of separation—of independently conceived strategy and consequent organization. It was primarily a co-operative force designed to facilitate the operations of ground units. As long as it acted as a reconnaissance service or as a mobile air artillery, clearing the roads for the panzer divisions, it was strikingly suc-

[9] De Seversky, *Atlantic Monthly*, March 1942.

cessful. The compact power of the "fighter team" as a
slugging, aggressive, land-gaining unit, hid from view
the distinct limitations of German air strength, its deficiencies in armament, speed and range, armor and
maneuverability—its lack of solidly trained personnel, and its inexperience in terms of independent operations.

The Germans had practically no familiarity with
long-range operations and this incapacity was to tell
heavily in the Battle of Britain. Even worse, they knew
nothing of the fine detail of night work, possessing
neither the personnel nor the training for this particular task. The leaders of the *Luftwaffe*, omnipotent on
land, floundered from one failure to another when
faced with a campaign entirely on their own resources
in the air.

The Royal Air Force on the other hand, though
without any of the peculiar strength of an air force
built to co-operate in a Stuka-panzer-artillery-infantry
team, had none of its limitations either. Neither in its
training, structure, nor equipment was it fettered by
the minds of men who saw it useful only as an adjunct to a ground army. Its philosophy of attack was
developed by brilliant airmen who had their own representation in the British Cabinet, and who did not
hesitate to vie with the other Services for anything
they considered vital to the well-being of their own
particular arm.

Its crews were trained in every aspect of individual
guerrilla warfare, as well as being organized to the last
detail for aerial team combat, a training which was
soon to tell its own story. They had had long experi-

ence in strategy and tactics in a continuous stream of
action all over the globe—in Palestine, Iraq, Hadrau-
mut, and the wilderness of north India. Whether in
an orderly formation or a free-for-all scuffle, they understood perfectly the whole philosophy of arms as it
applied to the air. Even the silly effort at promoting
revolution in Germany, attempted earlier in the war
by the dropping of tons of leaflets, had had its bright
side since it created the best group of night-flying
pilots and navigators in existence, a knot of alert, competent hit-and-run hunters to which the Germans had
nothing which could remotely compare.

Also, the British possessed a magnificent air-ground
co-operation system of another sort, whose purpose
was to service aerial operations exclusively. It was part
of a vast network of controlled defense, designed to
facilitate the new technique of cubic warfare and to
repel the expected vertical envelopment whose coming had long been apprehended by British air leaders.

Information concerning the approach of an enemy
was obtained by a superb radio-location and warning
system, so that he could be intercepted before reaching his target. The entire country was mapped out into
headquarters commands, group commands and sectors, each of which possessed a so-called "Operations"
Room. In these rooms were large maps on which details concerning enemy raids could be quickly shown
by various symbols, the aim being to give each Controller an identical picture of the progress of raids in
his own area. This information was relayed to Operations Rooms throughout the area simultaneously,
together with other applying information such as

weather data, location of squadrons, and particulars of such fighting as was taking place.

Equipped with this information, it was the Controller's job to estimate the speed of the raiders, to select a point where the foray could be intercepted and to put the necessary planes into the air. He had to make quick decisions so as to husband his resources and not risk being caught by succeeding waves of raiders with all his squadrons engaged elsewhere. The orders to fighters were issued by radio-telephone, utilizing latest information to put them in the best position for attack. Thus strict control was maintained over the fighters until the very moment when the enemy was sighted, after which they were on their own.

Without this complex and truly amazing system it would have been impossible to match the cunning and resources of a determined opponent capable of striking from almost any direction. Squadrons would have been scattered by innumerable feints, not knowing where the real raids were to take place, and would have found themselves either heavily outnumbered or with no enemy at all confronting them. Here was team work with a vengeance, of a kind that the Germans hardly expected.[10]

The British never risked their entire air armada in pitched battle anywhere, resting mainly on interception and attacking the invader piecemeal. Every artifice to entice the limited British force into an all-out encounter somewhere, so as to destroy their bases, failed no matter what beating their cities took. The

---

[10] A graphic detailed descriptive account may be found in the British Air Ministry's pamphlet, The Battle of Britain.

English simply would not rise to the bait. They could not be mangled on the ground since they had been at pains to scatter their planes in widely separated places —in fields, under hedges, and beneath haystacks.

The bases, ports, and headquarters themselves were not only dispersed but so camouflaged as to be virtually unrecognizable. Aircraft factories, in addition to being concealed and disguised, were decentralized into many manufacturing and assembly points, so that at no time could they be knocked out by a single blow.

The keynote to the whole British defense was flexibility plus co-ordinated action.

After a week of intensive struggle the Nazis found that they had lost almost 500 aircraft. In an additional two days some 245 aircraft more were added to the mounting toll. The British losses for this period were 153.

Rocked back by this unexpected resistance, the *Luftwaffe* halted to regroup itself and to take stock of its losses. It had learned that the familiar dive-bombing tactics practiced over France involved disastrous expenditures. After five days the Germans came into the attack once more, with the number of escorting fighters increased and the size of bomber formations reduced. The covering fighter screen now flew at great height, with the bombers also protected by lines of fighters fore and aft, above and below, in box formation. The area of attack was extended to include cities and aircraft factories, as well as fields and bases. London became the chief objective in an effort at terrorizing it into submission. The German planes came hurtling into the assault in waves of between forty to eighty, equally divided between bombers and accompanying fighters. British Spitfires and Hurricanes were thrown into the fray to intercept them before they could reach the city. Dog fights took place all over Southern England.

On the seventh of September some 350 German planes attempted to dash up the Thames estuary. Very few got through to the capital; the rest were met over the meadows of Kent and East Surrey and hurled back. More than 100 Nazi machines failed to return to their bases.

On the fifteenth of September the final large-scale effort was made by the Nazi command when 500 aircraft attempting to run the blockade of Hurricanes and Spitfires left 185 of their number in wreckage. The cost to the British had been only twenty-five planes. This triumph established beyond question the absolute British dominance of the skies over Britain.

There were a number of other great daylight raids and a stream of night-time incursions but the final result was already marked. The Germans attempted every type of arrangement and tactics cunning and rage could improvise. As many as five Messerschmitts sometimes accompanied a single bomber. They tried great night attacks and the use of converted Messerschmitts as fighter-bombers for daylight sorties, but the English defense remained impregnable.

It is interesting to note that the Italians, toward the tail end of this struggle, apprehensive lest they be denied the glory of being in on the kill, sent a number of planes into the attack. Their fighters were of an obsolete and poor type, though their bombers were somewhat more modern. Says Garnett: "They were greeted with almost incredulous enthusiasm by the pilots of the British fighter squadron which intercepted them in the Thames estuary. In a combat lasting only a few minutes, they shot down seven of the bombers and six of the fighters with no loss to themselves." [11] A few days later the surviving Italians made their second appearance, losing seven more aircraft, without a casualty on the British side. After this warm reception they failed to appear again. Apparently they had gone home.

In its practical sense the German adventure was ended. The English had suffered badly—parts of London were battered to a pulp; Manchester, Plymouth, and Coventry were horribly mangled. Over 14,000 Britons had been killed and 20,000 injured—the great bulk of these, civilians. But the triumphant *Luftwaffe*, the pride of the German war machine, had been turned back. That great grinding juggernaut on wheels, the German *Wehrmacht*, which had smashed irresistibly through Belgium, Luxembourg, the Netherlands, and France in nine weeks, was completely and effectually halted by a narrow body of water it could not bridge.

In this battle the German *Luftwaffe* lost some 2400 aircraft and 6000 trained men, an expenditure it could ill afford. The British losses by comparison were small. According to a statement issued by the Air Ministry they consisted of 733 planes, and 375 pilots killed and wounded.

[11] *War in the Air*, p. 198.

This fantastic struggle conducted three, four, five and often six miles above the ground, was the turning point of the war. Had the *Luftwaffe* prevailed Hitler could have destroyed the cities, factories, and communications of Great Britain at his leisure. Obtaining a bridgehead and occupying England and its sister island, Eire, would have been only a matter of weeks. The exultant Nazi would have stood like a great bird of prey, completely triumphant on the Continent, with only two obstacles between him and dominion of the earth. One of these, the great Soviet Bear, would have waited in the fullness of time until the Nazi appetite was ready for him. The other was the huge, rich, and indolent United States of America, immersed in internal bickering and dissension, incurably pacifist, and from the Nazi view a great, fat cow ripe for the slaughter.

Had Hitler triumphed in Britain, his strategy would have passed into a new phase—that of the long-awaited war of continents. There would have been the usual prelude—the heavy propaganda barrages attempting to dissolve American unity and to divide the nation into discordant and jangling groups, the substitution of diabolically conceived issues for the normal processes of democratic contention, and if possible the creation of revolution and chaos.

Independent of the success of such a campaign, all that would have stood between us and a hungry Nazi Europe would have been our Atlantic fleet. The Nazis were prepared to build a huge invading air force to serve as a cover for an enormous sea armada. With all Europe and Britain under their control, the Germans would have possessed shipbuilding facilities which would have enabled them to outbuild us on the ocean by at least five to one. Had they been able to take over Britain by a suborned government, as they have Norway and France, we should have been in the following situation: [12]

	United States	German Controlled
Battleships	15	29
Aircraft Carriers	6	9
Cruisers	37	93
Destroyers	159	440
Submarines	105	262
Total	322	833

These figures do not take into consideration the Japanese naval establishment, nor the fleet of the Netherlands and the other smaller countries of Europe.

The same comparative figures would unquestionably have held in relation to the mercantile tonnage required to transport a huge invading army to our shores.

During this period our capacity to defend ourselves against the oncoming Germans, had they been able to move an army of half a million men against us, would have been no greater than that of the Aztecs against Cortez, or the Incas against the mailed wrath of Pizarro.

It takes very little imagination to visualize the debt every American owes to these few thousand British youngsters who stopped the invading barbarian in the

[12] Based on estimates as of January 1941.

great amphitheaters of air over southern England and Wales. The beautiful homage paid them by Mr. Churchill will live as long as bravery and freedom and gallantry are known:

"The gratitude of every home in our Island, in our Empire, and indeed throughout the world, except in the abodes of the guilty, goes out to the British airmen who, undaunted by odds, unwearied in their constant challenge and mortal danger, are turning the tide of world war by their prowess and by their devotion. Never in the field of human conflict was so much owed by so many to so few."

The Battle of Britain proved conclusively that even in its present stage of development air power alone can be a decisive factor in the affairs of nations. It gave rise to a situation which may be accepted as doctrinal —that vast armies equipped with great quantities of armored machines operating with strong air units as an invincible team, are only valuable where they face an opponent on a contiguous land surface, where his industries, cities, air fields, and railroad centers are open to attack and may be occupied. Wherever an un-bridgeable body of water separates such a conqueror from his prey, the striking power of his military establishment becomes nullified. Possession of these enormous armies may even be an actual burden, limiting his freedom of action and approach. The opponent himself is impregnable to attack if he possesses a fighter force capable of coping with such enemy aircraft as may be thrown against him. The struggle then becomes one of air power alone, which without the intervention of surface arms, is quite capable of deciding the conflict.

This historic battle also gives rise to two other inferential conclusions:

One, that air power is used most economically not as a self-limited adjunct to some surface body, but as a completely self-contained apparatus possessing its own individuality of tactics, strategy, and structure. Not only unity of command but full representation at the very seat of political power is essential to its healthy development.

Two, that there is a limit to the energy, factory space, intelligence, and raw materials in any country, and that if an overwhelming proportion of these are drained off into equipping and maintaining other forces, it will be at the expense of the maturing air arm. It is obviously impossible for any nation to be as potent in all branches of military power as it would be if it concentrated all its efforts in the single avenue of approach where its advantage is the greatest. The conditions which force this conclusion are dominated by time, resources, and geography.

III

The great organic changes in the composition of armed bodies, induced by the advent of the aerial age, have affected equally the struggle for control over the no-man's waste of sea. Navies are now in the throes of the greatest revolutionary ferment in their history, a radical revision of function which is keeping pace in ratio to the emergence of the new ruling form, air power.

The history of great empires has been a history of sea power, of enduring control over the broad highways of ocean which link the mighty cities of the world. Over these ageless routes has flowed an unending stream of sea-borne caravans, of manufactured goods and raw materials, and fighting men bent on conquest. Every conqueror in history has aspired to control of these great brooding, mysterious areas of brine from whose bosom mastery of the earth could be grasped.

The authority which these expanses have always exercised over the affairs of men was described by the brilliant American admiral, Mahan, in cold precise words for the benefit of rulers, politicians, and their military stewards, in his classic work *The Influence of Sea Power upon History*. Nothing inferred by the rise of air power alters the validity of Mahan's doctrines, which apply today more accurately than ever. It is still true that whoever controls the sea lanes will control the world—though there is a notable difference in technique. Previously this had been done by dominating the little fringes of land which bordered the oceans. Today it is only possible by controlling the air over the oceans themselves.

The day of the surface vessel as possessing the sole initiative of action on the seas is finished. This initiative is passing in rapid transition stages to patrolling and raiding aircraft.

Thus we see a picture of surface sea power rapidly transmuting itself into the air, like a caterpillar emerg-

ing into another stage of its existence. The first nation
to accelerate this process by devoting its resources to
solving the question of air power will automatically
resolve the question of sea power. Even today no vessel
in existence can remain afloat against the threat of un-
contested air mastery, neither the heavily plated capital ships nor the ore boats which ply their way in the
semi-landlocked safety of the Skagerrak, the Kattegat,
and the Baltic, nor the oil-hauling barges on the interior rivers of the Continent.

Surface vessels, no matter how brilliantly handled,
cannot struggle against a superior force or weapons of
annihilating energy, novelty, and mobility. They may
no longer approach a shore held by powerful land-
based aircraft without risking the most disastrous consequences.

The task of fighting ships is now largely restricted
to convoying in waters safely beyond the range of
shore-based airplanes. As the latter's radius of action
develops, it is even conceivable that air power will
drive sea power under water altogether, as a furtive
and skulking adjunct to the aerial establishment.

If this should eventuate, as some aeronautical engineers are inclined to believe, the aircraft carrier, so essential in global operations today, would cease to have
a function. It is vulnerable to attack by submarines
and opposing aircraft. If military aviation is still evolving in a continuously lengthening radius of action, the
sea-based air field will inevitably disappear as having
outlived its usefulness.

However this may be in the future, the part played

by the carrier at the moment is an important one. It completely commands its own areas of action. The situation may be more readily grasped in its real aspects when it is realized that the aircraft carrier has an artillery range of some 300 miles from its center. Thus it can shoot down surface opponents several hundred miles away, while these in turn can only attack what may be considered to be the carrier's expendable ammunition.

Even before the events at Pearl Harbor and the South Pacific established the torpedo plane as the foremost enemy of floating craft, airplanes had radically changed the nature of naval engagements. Previous to December 1941, aerial bombs had sunk sixty-seven British naval vessels. Fifty-two were accounted for by mines and twenty-four by torpedoes, ten of which were loosed from planes. Only eight were sent down as a result of naval gunfire. Since that time the arc of loss by aerial assault has sharply risen, accounting in a few months for the death of more fighting ships than all causes in World War I put together.

Like the Seminole Indian who had to take to his inaccessible swamps to escape the encroachments of the white man, surface naval vessels are compelled to retire to the distant safety of the ocean roadways. They may no longer venture out without a guard of fighter planes, nor may they approach a strongly held shore. The first clear-cut test of strength between dominant surface power and the blustering ships of the air, in which the challenge was thrown and the issue settled once and for all, occurred in the Battle of Norway.

The campaign in Norway was a direct result of the British attempt to cut the shipping lines which tied Germany to her source of Swedish iron ore, amounting at that time to over seventy-five per cent of the Reich's imports.

Under the supreme leadership of General von Falkenhorst, the Germans struck with a lightning thrust on April 9, 1940. Troopships disguised as merchantmen lay in the Norwegian harbors. Under an awning of planes still other troop carriers led by big battleships raced to the key ports on Norway's coast. At the same time great squadrons of troop-carrying aircraft shuttled back and forth over the Skagerrak, landing picked troops together with their equipment.

Working in perfect co-ordination, the Germans quickly improvised air fields. Oslo and the cities to the south fell into the Nazi grasp almost at once. Within a few days the Germans, moving by sea, air, and land, had pushed on to Trondheim and beyond, and had occupied virtually the entire coast.

Never before in history had an overseas expeditionary force departed from its bases without complete naval control of the intervening sea routes. With royal contempt for this holy ordination the Germans placed a fully equipped army division on wings and moved it to its destination within a few hours. In one single and continuous operation fifteen thousand Teuton warriors "with full field equipment, supplies, ammunition, machine guns, and Rheinmetal 37 millimeter anti-aircraft guns, plus artillery, were flown from German bases and landed in the invaded country." [13]

[13] Williams, *Airpower*, pp. 368, 369.

The British immediately parried this audacious move by bringing in their fleet and investing the waters of the North Sea and the Skagerrak. In a correlating action an Allied expeditionary force attempted a counter-invasion, striking in two great prongs, one south of the important port of Trondheim, and one to the north. By April 20 there were 50,000 French and British soldiers in Norway.

The Allied troop movements were protected by planes of the Fleet air arm which had taken off from carriers parked some 200 miles off shore. Here was the first genuine test of power between carrier and shore-based aircraft. The answer came swiftly. Within a few days most of the British planes assigned to this mission were destroyed, leaving the strategic heights of sky henceforward in the possession of the enemy.

Nazi warplanes swooped down in clouds on the unprotected French and English, bombing supplies and ships, and machine-gunning troops almost at will. Whole divisions were moved around as if on the back of some huge fabulous roc; and where no landing facilities existed, paratroopers were dropped into the narrow valleys to outflank the Allied position.

It was soon clear that the Allied counter-attack had fizzled out completely due to lack of mastery in the air, and that a further continuation of this unequal struggle would be suicidal. By May 2, all Allied forces south of Trondheim had been evacuated. On June 10 the last remnants of the British armies in the North, a thoroughly beaten force, finally withdrew.

At no time during this struggle was the British Navy able to fulfill its traditional mission by cutting the supply lines of the enemy and isolating his task forces. It could not prevent the hauling of materials and men across the sky-guarded waters of the Kattegat and Skagerrak. Neither was it able to protect the landing of its own troops despite the fact that the harbors were practically unfortified, the native population friendly, and the German invaders scattered in pockets over a wide area.

Shortly after the first crash of the charging German thunderbolt had given the *Luftwaffe* possession of northern bases, British ships found all the coastal seas of Norway unsafe: the hunter had been tragically transformed into the game and had to flee the vicinity.

The explanation of Prime Minister Churchill to Commons was dramatically simple. This disaster to the Allied arms, he said, was due to "intense continuous bombings of the bases at Namsos and Aandalsnes which prevented the landing of large reinforcements, and even of artillery for the infantry already landed. It therefore was necessary to withdraw the troops or to leave them to be destroyed by overwhelming forces."

At Norway it was demonstrated that battleships no longer could land men on a hostile shore unless they were able to achieve absolute control of the skies over the point of entry. It was shown, also, that sea-based aviation is not capable of competing with the heavier, faster, and more numerous craft of a competent land-based adversary.

The rising authority of the airplane as possessor of the capacities for initiative and surprise was brought out at the Battle of Taranto.

This engagement which took place at the toe of
Italy on November 13, 1940, is noteworthy not only
because it marked a complete victory by aircraft over
sea power, but because the planes used were relatively
obsolete Fairey Swordfish, a type which does no more
than 160 miles an hour. These ancient craft, taking off
from British carriers, succeeded in sinking a 35,000-ton
Italian battleship, a capital ship of smaller tonnage,
two cruisers, two fleet auxiliaries, and some other vessels. All this was accomplished with the loss of only
two airplanes, despite the fact that the harbor was protected by the most modern ground defenses to be had.

A study of this exploit should have prepared us for
such a surprise assault as that which took place at
Pearl Harbor. Granting the element of surprise, any
type of torpedo or bomb carrier, obsolescent or not,
can sink any ship afloat. The weakness of these airplanes is against other and superior airplanes—not
against battleships and cruisers.

The noteworthy factor involved in the disaster at
Pearl Harbor was not the Japanese success—that was,
under the circumstances, inevitable. Nor was it the
treachery of the Japanese—the possibility of such an
occurrence has been distinctly in the military mind for
a long time.[14] The fact of striking importance which
emerges is that for the first time naval power deliber-

[14] According to Pearson and Allen (*Washington Merry-Go-
Round*, February 28, 1942) Lieut. General Arnold, Chief of the
Army Air Forces, told officials of the Insular Affairs Bureau back in
1939 that if he were an enemy he would like the assignment of
bombing Pearl Harbor. He pointed out that the navy was huddled
close in the harbor, and the harbor's mouth was narrow making it
difficult to get out, and that it was a perfect target for an air attack.

ately was used as auxiliary to air power. The United Nations were totally unprepared for this occurrence and for the events which followed it. They seemed to be completely unaware that a new instrument of power had been introduced, and were not in a position anywhere in the Pacific to undertake an effective defense.[15]

Observers are unanimous in the opinion that a few hundred Wellingtons or B-17's with a hauberk of modern pursuit ships used in time would have stopped the Japanese cold in their tracks. One of the basic elements which differentiates the strategy of air attack from that of the older military institutions is that in the case of the former the time and space elements are of infinitely greater importance. Fifty planes used at the moment of stress are worth 1000 brought up later when the enemy has had a chance to entrench

[15] At a time when almost everyone sadly misjudged the Japanese as foemen to be respected, treating with them as if they were only a peg or two above the painted spearmen of Somaliland, "Billy" Mitchell made what turned out to be an exact and proper estimate of their abilities. The following is an abstract of testimony given on June 1, 1933, before a joint Congressional committee to investigate dirigible disasters:

"Rep. Delaney: What is the attitude of the Japanese with regard to flying?

"Gen. Mitchell: They know the value of air power and they are working as hard on it as anybody else.

"Rep. Delaney: They have not been successful in their experiments with lighter than air and heavier than air.

"Gen. Mitchell: They have been extremely successful with everything they have tried. They have an excellent air force.

"Rep. Delaney: My information is that the Japanese mind is not formed to absorb this information.

"Gen. Mitchell: That is not so. They are excellent airmen in every way, shape and form. I have been with them. I know they are good."

himself, erect his bases and establish his lines of supply.

Lieutenant Governor Van Mook of the Dutch East Indies declared that 200 airplanes would have made Java invincible. Admiral Fiske wrote that fifty torpedo planes for attack upon Japanese troopships and fifty pursuits to deal with their air units might have prevented Japanese landings in the Philippines.[16] American and British experts in Malaya were unanimous in the belief that a few squadrons of modern bombing and fighting planes would have spelled the difference between victory and defeat, preventing completely the subsequent Japanese southward movement. According to Lieutenant General George Brett, American flyers in Java took out our few big bombers daily, not knowing whether any landing field would be left when they returned to their base.

All this was the result of a curious military blind-spot, of an insistent inertia, and a smug lack of accommodation to a new circumstance whose coming had been heralded with a blare of trumpets over two years of bitter war.

In Manila the clear-sighted MacArthur was vainly demanding airplanes. He had read the auguries of the times and was ill at ease. In Hawaii the heads of the military and naval establishments, secure in the great power of American might, patiently awaited the political decisions by which their actions were regulated. The Dutch East Indies, acutely aware of the nature of the terrible danger which was impending, were send-

[16] *Liberty*, March 28, 1942.

ing missions to Washington and, like MacArthur, begging for airplanes.

In England the warnings of the R.A.F. leaders that Malaya and Singapore were resting on a defense which had no more value under modern conditions than if it were made of tissue paper, went completely unheeded. The aloof British Colonials and their Tory partisans in the bureaus of Whitehall had managed to learn absolutely nothing from the experiences of this war—not even from the classic epic which became known later as the Battle of Britain. They believed the Malayan jungle to be "impenetrable," an error comparable to that of the French who had considered the Argonne Forest an insuperable barrier to serious military operations. The keynote to their defense of the entire South Pacific area was Singapore, a base which they considered impregnable. The guns defending it were supposed to be the heaviest in existence and were on fixed emplacements facing the sea. Its anti-aircraft installations were called "unparalleled." It never occurred to these men that the attack might be directed from overhead, co-ordinated with a flanking operation through the rice fields of Indo-China and Thailand at the back door.

"Fifteen years ago," commented Viscount Trenchard ruefully, "I, as Chief of the Air Staff, was advocating that Malaya should be made a great air base, and that our limited allotment of money should be spent on bombers and torpedo aircraft instead of on the huge guns that are there now." However, nothing could move the Government from a dogmatic reliance on the type of fixed fortification which had served the Empire so well in the past.

The situation throughout this gigantic area, by which the United Nations forfeited resources tragically required for their own war effort, was exactly like that of Norway, and was repeated from island to island. Tremendous air squadrons knocked out the few Allied planes. Dive-bombers then completed the job, allowing the sea-borne forces to move in and take over. What might easily have been was indicated in the slashing triumph of American and Australian air forces striking at Jap invasion bases in New Guinea on March 18, 1942. Twenty-three Japanese ships including twelve warships were sunk or damaged, with small Allied losses.

The fallacious concepts by which the blind led the blind in the upper echelons of British leadership is outlined in Churchill's statement to Commons after the great battleships, *Prince of Wales* and *Repulse*, had been sent to the bottom by Japanese torpedo planes off the Malay coast.[17] He declared: "These two fast powerful ships constituted an essential feature in our plans for meeting the new Japanese danger. . . ."

A more intelligible view was taken by de Seversky, who complained to the writer: "Here I go to a lot of trouble to write a whole chapter to prove exactly how airplanes could sink battleships and then the Japanese

[17] It is curious that the torpedo planes which struck this blow were British in design, a Blackburn model built under license in Japan.

go and sink the *Repulse* and *Prince of Wales* and I have to throw the chapter out." [18]

The unqualified superiority of the land-based airplane as an instrument of battle was unmistakably shown at the battles of Midway and the Coral Sea. These two struggles will go down in naval history as milestones in the evolution of sea war and the historic processes of sea-borne invasions.

In the Coral Sea battle, the first Japanese naval defeat in history, the struggle developed in its first phase into an out-and-out contest between aircraft carriers. It ended with the appearance of General MacArthur's big bombers from Australia, which forced the withdrawal of the Japanese Navy, after it had taken a heavy drubbing. Rear Admiral Frederick C. Sherman who commanded the U. S. carrier *Lexington,* which was sunk in this engagement, stated that it "signaled a new kind of warfare at sea and was as much a turning point as the battle between the *Monitor* and the *Merrimac*."

At the Coral Sea it was emphasized that sea-borne aircraft were no match for land-based planes, and that the carriers themselves were as vulnerable as any other vessel to attack from the skies.

All this was underscored with rigid finality in the spectacular American triumph at Midway, early in June, 1942. Midway spotlighted for even the most

[18] The torpedoing of five battleships in a row within a few days of each other, two British, two American and one Japanese, ended forever the argument, which arose after "Billy" Mitchell's practice-sinking of the captured German warships in 1921, as to whether airplanes could actually sink battleships under combat conditions.

myopic eyes the plight of invading armadas which venture within the jurisdictional area of shore-based demolition planes. In this great victory is contained a grim note of warning that the day of invading sea armadas is finished *and that there are no enabling factors which would render success more likely for us than it was for Admiral Yamamoto in his attempt to take our island outposts in the Pacific.*

The Japs came in with the largest concentration of surface ships and aircraft carriers ever sent forth on any mission in this war. The formula was identical with that used so successfully in the assault on the unprotected Indies and Malay States. Confidently Japanese Zero fighters appeared over Midway, strafing and bombing but carefully avoiding hitting the airfield runways, apparently expecting to occupy the islands without undue difficulty and to utilize them as bases for a progressive extension of their attacks on other U. S. possessions.

First contact with the enemy was made by Army bombers ranging far over the ocean on the afternoon of June 3. The following morning Navy and Marine dive-bombers and torpedo carriers together with big four-motored Army B-17-E's came roaring out of the sun. Still other long-range military craft joined them from Hawaii, 1,200 miles to the southeast and from Johnson Island. Whole squadrons of Flying Fortresses had a go at the startled Japs.

Totally unprepared for this reception, the Zeros soon withdrew from the assault on Sand and Eastern Islands (which together comprise Midway), and turned, in an ineffectual effort to protect their own ships and host vessels which were desperately zigzagging to avoid the merciless beating our planes were giving them.

When the battle ended, the debris of Japanese fighter planes lay littered over the green waters of the Pacific. Every one of the five carriers which had accompanied the Jap task force had been hit. Four were known to have been sunk, together with 275 aircraft. All told, some twenty-one Japanese fighting ships and troop transports were crippled or sent to the bottom as the proud armada turned from its mission of conquest and fled for its life.

The Battle of Midway was a battle of aircraft. At no time did any of the contending surface vessels come within a day's journey of each other.

IV

German operations in the Mediterranean Island of Crete revealed to startled military soothsayers still another new plateau of action. They demonstrated, among other things, the complete soundness of the old Russian and German theses relative to gliders, and rounded out the concept of the strategic mission of air-borne troops. For the future they point to the complete freedom of invading armies from orthodox types of land and sea communications.

In this minor contest, which is more an incident than a battle, is presaged the technique and strategy of intercontinental war of the future—its emancipation from the chains of linear dimensions, its ability to create its own automatic supply lines in which distance and terrain will no longer be governing factors, and its fantastic capacity for concentration of superior and overwhelming force *in any portion of the globe from any given point.*

The strategy is already here. It only waits on technical development to bring it to a head.

The Battle of Crete must be understood in these terms: It was not an air expedition alone, but an air, land, and naval contest in which all other services were engaged auxiliary to air power.

The island of Crete, which forms a barrier across the entrance to the Aegean Sea, was thought to present unsurmountable difficulties to any plan of attack. It was separated from the European mainland by a gap of water 150 miles wide securely held under the big guns of the Royal Navy and a limited group of squadrons of the R.A.F. It was occupied by some 45,000 seasoned British troops. Local topographical conditions were extremely unfavorable to movement, the island consisting of the upper levels of a range of mountains rising out of the Mediterranean, its passes connected by high, rough saddles. Very few flat areas exist and the road system is extremely primitive.

Secure in the apparent safety of distance, the English had prepared no defenses and there were no secret or camouflaged air fields which could be easily defended. The main squadrons of the British air arm were at Alexandria, 340 miles away.

The attack was sprung, on May 20, 1941, with all the electric qualities of surprise and shock, although the British had known for days that some type of German assault was brewing. Operations started in the small hours of the morning, with airplanes dropping flares, shrieking Stukas roaring down on ground objectives, and big new Messerschmitts spewing their murderous fire in every direction. The object was to confuse the defenders and cripple as many R.A.F. planes on the ground as possible, knock out anti-aircraft defenses, and force the abandonment of the three main landing fields.

Some time after dark a fleet of several hundred Ju-52 and Focke-Wulf transports swept in over the Cannea-Malemi-Suda Bay area, each carrying a complement of fully equipped parachutists. Other planes dropped machine guns, ammunition, and light mortars. These were assembled by the paratroopers, who immediately took to cover in prepared bomb craters, and waited. By dawn some 5000 Germans had been landed at key objectives, holding positions around the air fields at Rethymnos, Candia, and Malemi, and seizing the harbor at Suda Bay so as to eliminate it as a base for fleet operations.

Synchronized with this movement, great waves of transports began to arrive towing trains of gliders tandem fashion like boxcars, carrying Austrian Alpine units especially trained to deal with rough mountainous country. These succeeded in occupying the principal air field, at Malemi, a development which turned out to be the pivotal action of the Cretan campaign.

During the critical phase of the battle, German ground troops were restricted to light equipment and armament, but had at their disposal the unlimited resources of the 8th German Air Corps. Protecting their advance were the familiar light bombers which acted as an accompanying artillery. Here we have a case of a lightly armed infantry advancing behind an overwhelming artillery barrage and acting at the same time as a principal auxiliary to a dominant air operation.

The entire assault was timed with the precision of clockwork. The first shower of paratroopers had seized the air fields almost at once, depriving the British of sorely needed bases. Overhead protection for the defenders virtually ceased to exist, and after the third day of fighting, the R.A.F. was forced to announce its withdrawal from the island altogether.

Once the Germans controlled the coastal roads and main air fields, they placed the narrow neck of channel water under a heavy cross-fire from the skies, making it altogether unsafe for the British fleet stationed there. After severe losses, including the sinking of two cruisers and four destroyers, the fleet was compelled to abandon the Aegean zone to the Germans who at once established communications with the island directly by sea.

The fifth day of the invasion, Crete came into German hands except for continued guerrilla fighting in the interior. The *Luftwaffe* had brought in some 38,000 men—a contingent equal to the sum total of our Continental Armies of the Revolutionary War. There were about 7800 casualties, and a loss of some 290 planes.

Crete was the first instance of a true air-borne invasion. The Germans utilized the airplane for everything. They dropped men, howitzers, machine guns, motorcycles, light tanks, and artillery. They landed shock troops, engineers, and mountain infantry—including specialized groups whose whole function was to remove the debris of wrecked planes, so as to clear the landing fields for subsequent operations.

This campaign marked the end of an era in warmaking and the beginning of a new one.

IV. THE AXIS PLAN OF STRATEGY

THE situation of the United Nations in this conflict, if it is to be determined by the horn-book of military convention, is not good.

The Allies are forced to operate along the circumference of two enormous circles and are thus by the very nature of their strategical position forced into a dissipation of their available resources. The initiative of action, as well as choice of position, resides with the Axis powers who may strike quickly and with crushing strength in any direction, along a network of securely held lines.

The military policy of the Axis has been dominated progressively since the passage of the Lease-Lend Act by the vast industrial potentials in the possession of the American nation. If American factory facilities are to be allowed a free rein in the production of guns, munitions and war-making machines, the ultimate margin of superiority would be so overwhelming that any unconquered area, China, Persia, India, or Portugal, could serve as a stepping-off place for a specially designed American variety of blitz attack.

The strategy of the Axis in consequence of these factors, which they clearly understand, moves irresistibly in one direction—not the immediate conquest of America but its isolation from the rest of the world.

Their scheme is to immobilize us by forcing us on the defensive; to cut our supply lines to China, Russia, and Britain; and to place us on an *ersatz* basis in reference to certain essential raw materials which are either not produced on our continent or not sufficiently abundant, thus hampering our productive capacities.

A primary consideration in the minds of the Axis leaders is the need for guaranteed access to the earth's basic resources. The first leg of the journey was successfully undertaken by Japanese conquest of the Dutch East Indies, giving control of an almost inexhaustible supply of oil, rubber, tin, and other basic materials. When the entire chain of action is complete, the Axis will not only have broken the United Nations' blockade but will actually have placed England and the Americas under a counter-blockade of its own.

The Axis will attempt first to stabilize the Russian front, unless the Soviets show sufficient power to make this phase impossible. Germany and its European partners will seek to move at the same time along North Africa to Suez and through Turkey and the Caucasus to the Middle East. The Japanese task on this timetable is to move simultaneously on India, the plan calling for a juncture of the Axis allies somewhere in the center of Asia. The appointed action against Australia during this period would be simply an intimidating one directed against its northern fringe, the object being to wall the great sub-continent off from the battle arenas of Asia, neutralizing it as an important combat force. As time went on, the great Anglo-Saxon domain "down under" would be forced to adjust itself to the Axis program or perish.

In consequence of this immense maneuver, the African continent would fall automatically.

This would leave the Axis powers not only in military contact but with access to practically every raw material whose exploitation was necessary for the unlimited expansion of their military forces.

Experience has proven that the conquered are as often governed by expediency as they are by heroism. Just as Thailand lent herself to the designs of the Japanese, and Vichy France flung herself into the arms of the truculent Nazi, the voice of opportunism would speak to the millions of China and India. To India in particular it would mean little more than a change in overlords, and the presence of a self-evident *fait accompli* could be relied on to bring the realistic Chinese finally in line. A great spate of propaganda aimed against the white man as the source of all evil would find an increasing acceptance among the dark masses of Asia. The slogan of the *Dai Asia Kyoki*,[1] "Asia for the Asiatics," would gain magically in hypnotic quality as the white *sahib* retreated step by step from his strongholds on the great continent.

None of this would disturb the realistic thinking of the Nazis in the slightest. They already represent themselves as the champion of the dark Mohammedan masses of Egypt, Arabia, and the Middle East,

[1] Great Asia Association.

and regard the whole maneuver as one of ordinary expediency on the road to conquest.[2]

With the liquidation of resistance in Asia, the Russian giant would find himself squeezed on all sides and would be given the choice of coming into the Axis or of being squashed in a huge envelopment operating along his whole 6400 miles of waterline and 6950 miles of land border.[3] What the political hierarchy which controls the Soviet Union would do under these circumstances is anybody's guess, but the final result would add to the same total under any circumstance and would be inevitable.

If this great plan can be made good, the collapse of England and Ireland are foregone conclusions, thus depriving us of the dagger pointed straight at the heart of Hitler which is now at our disposal.

The Axis scheme of battle would be then to place our entire continent under a state of siege with the major tactics those of attrition.

Peace would be offered on the basis of the *status quo* to allow Germany and Japan a period of quiet in which to digest their gains and adjust their military economies to the rich and virtually exhaustless assets at their disposal. At the same time the ravaging tactics of psychological assault will be resumed, aided by ex-

[2] How all this works out in practice may be seen in the actual application of Nazi race theories. Where Jews and Poles, who are as blonde as the Germans themselves, are acted against as subhumans of inferior species, the Japanese are considered by German law racially equal to the Teuton. There is no crime or stigma attached to the marriage between a German woman and a Japanese man, while such a marriage contracted with a Jew or Pole would mean disgrace and prison.

[3] This is exclusive of the Northern coast of 3800 miles.

ternal pressure on our commercial and industrial economies so as to soften us up and make us amenable to
an Axis offer. In addition to attempting to foment
dangerous dissensions within our own borders Hitler
would make ingenious use of the Pan-Spanish aspira-
tions of the Falangists, in an effort to create revolutionary uprisings throughout South America.

If we refused the proffered bait the Barbarian Horde
would attempt to obtain a foothold on the big bulge
in Brazil from which to begin a land campaign. If we
were to take over Latin America bodily as a necessary
measure of defense, the Axis would concentrate the
massed resources of three continents on the most enormous sea and air strength they could construct, feinting and striking in all directions, and content to wait
a generation if necessary to bring us to heel.

In the event England were conquered and the British Government attempted to carry on the war from
Canada in conjunction with the United States, "the
population of the British Isles would be subjected to
deliberate progressive starvation as hostages." The German idea is that Washington and Ottawa would capitulate before allowing the people of those islands to
be starved to death to the last man, woman, and
child. [4]

The single factor basic to Axis strategy and utterly

[4] Joseph C. Harsch, *Pattern of Conquest*, pp. 211, 213. Harsch
refers to the plan for starving Britain as "ordinary matter-of-fact conversation of everyday Berlin. . . . That the Germans are capable of
doing it is not a far stretch of imagination. They not only could,
but actually plan to do it if that becomes necessary to achieve their
objective." The Germans are already using food as an instrument of
state policy and employ deliberate mass starvation on a large scale in
Poland to achieve political results.

necessary to the successful completion of their plan of world conquest is an America on the defensive building up a huge army which it cannot use abroad, or sending its reserves off to be slaughtered in widely separated places.

The entire Nazi scheme of action, together with the rich success which has already attended its operations, may be seen in a few ordinary facts and some simple arithmetical computations.

Economists of the old school, and other learned authorities, have pointed out tirelessly that Germany and Japan were ill-equipped to fight a long war—that they were impoverished, had neither resources nor purchasing power, and must in the long run collapse through sheer hunger and a leaching of their physical assets.

This concept of the world we live in is a blunder which can have the most disastrous consequences. It is based on the same type of miscalculation which caused us to sequester all the gold and silver we could get our hands on at artificially pegged prices and bury it in the ground at Fort Knox. Had we bought scrap iron or magnesium, as the Japanese did, and buried that in the ground, it would have been infinitely sounder economics. The power of gold as an arbitrator of human affairs has virtually disappeared. It no longer dictates the course of war and the supplying of armies. The new economic strategy makes it possible simply to absorb the resources of the state, or those of conquered areas, without reference to the fine legalities of purchase. The success of the Soviet in building its industries despite a want of capital, brings to the fore the newest measurement in wealth: man-hours.

The ability to conscript labor and levy on property and wealth gives absolute assurance of increasing resistance power to the expanding totalitarian states. The key to this economy is the enslavement of vanquished populations and the looting on a grand scale of their resources. Thus all the states Germany and Japan have captured have been put to work for the conqueror, digging his coal, smelting his ore, growing his foodstuffs, and building his instruments of war.

The Axis, instead of growing weary with further conquest, is like a giant anaconda which waxes fatter and stronger with each victim ingested. The capture of new territories enables it to finance its further operations on a continually growing scale. And by this series of forced marches the Axis is rapidly usurping control of critical materials whose lack may be expected to seriously cripple our own industrial war machine. We have already become a have-not nation in regard to such commodities as rubber and silk, causing a vital readjustment in our entire pattern of activity. Even a scarcity of minor metals whose names still sound exotic to the public ear, may have grave consequences. In modern metallurgy the key to successful production is the alloy material. Our tremendous iron and steel output becomes meaningless without such elements as manganese and chromite, since without them hard steel for armor plate cannot be made. Without magnesium, highly stressed structural castings, which combine great lightness with rigidity, may not be fabricated.

The very nature of our factory and industrial civilization has made all the great nations of the West less and less self-sufficient and more and more dependent on outside sources of supplies. In the case of manganese we produce less than one per cent of the world's supply but use close to twenty-five per cent.[5] The same is true of nickel where we require half of the world's production to turn out our special steels and alloys, with only a few hundred tons available from American sources.[6] "Chromium, tungsten, antimony, tin, mica, and rubber are only a few of the raw materials indispensable to American production which come from ports halfway around the world."[7]

In 1941 there was an estimated domestic production in chromium of 10,000 tons against an import of 800,000 tons.[8] Ninety-eight per cent of the quinine consumed in the United States came from the East Indies, as did eighty-five per cent of its kapok and seventy-one per cent of its pepper.

Of the immense stocks of rubber we will require, fifty-five per cent came from British Malaya, thirty-one per cent from the Netherlands Indies, and six per cent from French Indo-China. Of the 124,810 long tons of tin imported in 1940, 96,454 came from the British Malay States and 12,101 from the nearby Neth-

[5] War Against Waste, issued by Office for Emergency Management.
[6] Luckily the largest part of our supply of this commodity comes from our neighbor to the north, Canada.
[7] War Against Waste.
[8] Twenty per cent came from the Philippine Islands, sixteen per cent from Turkey, forty-four per cent from Africa and eight per cent from Cuba.

erlands Indies.[9] By far the greater part of the tungsten
—a necessary element in the manufacture of high-speed
cutting tools and the filaments of light bulbs and
radio tubes—comes from China. There are impending
shortages of molybdenum, copper, zinc, lead, cobalt,
vanadium, and numerous other materials necessary
to the flow of the war effort.

Examining the ledger of Nazi economic strategy we
find that when the Germans took over Czechoslovakia
they gained with it a vast mining, steel, textile, and
chemical industry. The annual value of coal exports
alone exceeded $170,000,000. The great Czech steel
and engineering works were able to compete in the
world's markets on bridges, locomotives and railway
cars, automobiles, airplanes, armament, munitions, and
heavy machinery. The destruction of the small Slav
state left in the hands of Germany more than 1000
Czech tanks, many of the 80-ton type which were later
instrumental in beating the French and British, 1500
planes, and the entire war matériel of forty Czech divisions. More important, it handed into Nazi possession the famous Skoda Munitions Works which had
furnished most of the arms for the nations of the Balkans and Eastern Europe.

In the conquest of Austria, Germany gained iron
ore, timber, magnesite, and important factory facilities. In Poland she took over tremendous mineral resources, especially the coal and metal industries of
Silesia, as well as zinc, textiles, and timber.

The entire territory of Europe west of the Lenin-

[9] Our own production was forty-four tons, mostly from Alaska, although considerable native resources exist in Bolivia.

grad-Smolensk-Taganrog line is working for Germany. This includes the so-called allies of the Reich, Hungary, Rumania, Bulgaria, and Italy, as well as such neutrals as Sweden, whose entire output is directed into Axis hands. Hitler has managed to get control of nearly 260,000,000 people with a working force of something like 155,000,000. All of this tremendous array of industrial workers is laboring for German victory.

When the *Wehrmacht* overran Poland, Belgium, France, and Norway, it placed in Hitler's hands one-third of the world's zinc supply. With the conquest of France and Norway, Germany took control of the largest aluminum industry in the world.

The Third Reich picked up tremendous increases in iron and steel production in Belgium, France, Luxembourg, Poland, and Russia. This includes raw ore as well as the apparatus for processing finished equipment, particularly military appliances and machinery. She is now probably first in the world in armament-producing facilities. Germany found great electro-chemical industries in Belgium, France, and Norway. She obtained textiles in the Netherlands and France; heavy industrial equipment in Belgium, Luxembourg, the Netherlands, and Denmark; oil in Rumania, chromite in Jugoslavia, bauxite in Hungary, Norway, France, and Jugoslavia; lead, copper, zinc, and manganese in Jugoslavia and Austria; and artificial silk in France and the low countries. Together with her French reserves she now controls ninety-five per cent of the world's potash. She found great ways and yards for shipbuilding in France, the Netherlands, Denmark, and Norway, and extracts foodstuffs and dairy products from France, the Netherlands, Denmark, the Balkans, and Hungary.

In France the Reich took over such famed establishments as the Schneider-Creusot Works with its great production of artillery; and the giant factories of Renault, Farman, Citroen, Voisin, and Caudron, with their teeming output of armored cars, planes, engines, and tanks.

If Germany can pocket the Caucasus and the Near East, she will be no longer dependent on her hydrogenation plants for the production of synthetic oil. If she is able to conquer Africa she will receive boundless tribute in iron ore, phosphates, zinc, diamonds, copper, tin, petroleum, mica, graphite, vanadium, manganese, asbestos, coal, gold, textiles, cotton, hides, farm produce, and fish, animal and forest products.

The materials which fit into the critical category for Germany and which she has been unable to get from the overborne areas in her possession, are raw cotton, jute, rubber, nickel, tin, mica, antimony and tungsten. She undoubtedly has large stock piles of these. But whatever their magnitude, they are sooner or later bound to be used up. If the war is to be a long one, the Reich must establish a pipeline juncture with her partner in Asia from which she can siphon off into her own hungry industrial body the over-abundance of those materials now in Japanese hands.

The rewards which accrued to Japanese operations were fabulous and swift in coming. The Netherlands East Indies alone consist of 735,267 square miles of territory with a total population of 71,000,000. Counting the Philippines, British East Indies, Malaya, Thailand, and Burma, the Nipponese have seized within a few months an area as large as half the United States, containing magnificent resources, much of which is found nowhere else in significant quantity. The Japanese conquests, in fact, changed the strategic materials situation so radically that the Axis now controls ninety-one per cent of the world's rubber, seventy-three per cent of its tin, and sixty-six per cent of its bauxite.

In the Dutch East Indies there had been a production of 8,000,000 tons of oil of high quality. In British Borneo there were another 1,000,000 tons. Since Japan also holds the Burma fields, and operates those on the Russian island of Sakhalin as a Japanese concession, she now controls every source of petroleum in the Pacific.

In the former Dutch territory Japan secured a coal production of 2,000,000 tons annually, which could be vastly increased by tapping the virgin resources of Borneo and Sumatra. Anthracite also is found in French Indo-China and the Japs discovered great deposits in Manchukuo. It is estimated that at least 20,000,000,-000 tons exist there and it is now being taken out at the rate of some 35,000 tons a day. The Dutch Indies hold second place among all tin-yielding countries, the world's foremost production coming from the new Japanese possession of Malaya. This former British territory is also the top producer of rubber, but is almost matched by the Dutch Indies.

Japan, which had in 1940 a total aluminum production of 35,000 metric tons, inherited in the Indies a rapidly expanding tonnage of bauxite together with great electric power plants on the Asahan River to process it into aluminum. In Manchukuo are inexhaustible quantities of both bauxite and oil shale and there are reports that that country holds astronomical amounts of magnesite.

Japan's food supplies have been strengthened by its capture of the great rice fields of Indo-China, Thailand and Burma. The Dutch Indies export annually 1,180,-000 metric tons of sugar, 670,000 tons of cocoanut products, and over 100,000 tons of maize. In Manchukuo the Japs have found wheat. legumes, wool, hides, and meat.

In Borneo and the Celebes are several hundred million tons of iron ore, and nickel is present in the central and southeastern Celebes. The present production of 40,000 tons could be heavily increased without trouble. Java mines around 12,000 tons of manganese, an output which has been steadily increasing.

Many other industries exist in the Indies—chemical establishments, manufactories of cement, glass and rubber, oil refineries, paint and varnish industries, leather goods, paper mills, and a variety of other factories and workshops. There has been a considerable expansion in textiles and a steady growth of woodwork shops, shipbuilding and drydock companies, metal assembly plants, machine shops, and plants for the making of high octane gasoline.

Diamonds are mined in Borneo and sulphur in Java, Sumatra, and the Celebes. There are vast unexplored and unworked regions throughout the Indies which contain valuable deposits of iron ore, nickel, lead, zinc, sulphur, and copper, which the Japanese are certain to develop and exploit just as they have the iron, steel, and chemical industries of Manchukuo.

According to a report by the U. S. Bureau of Mines, the Axis is now almost evenly balanced against the Allies in vital metal supplies.

The progress of the Axis towards economic ascendancy may be seen in redistribution of the following key commodities since 1938:

Percentage of Axis Control of World Production

	1938	1942
Wool	3.4	12
Rubber	0	91.1
Flax	6.8	35.8
Cotton	0.8	2.6
Wood Pulp	11.4	32.9
Cement	33.7	51.6
Coal and Lignite	32	45.4
Crude Petroleum	0.4	6.7
Steel	24.7	43.1
Iron Ore	7.3	44.6
Manganese Ore	10	34.9
Nickel Ore	0	2.9
Copper Ore	6	9.1
Lead Ore	8.4	21.9
Zinc Ore	15	28.5
Tin Ore	9.4	73.2
Chrome Ore	2.7	16.9
Bauxite	25.2	65.8

These figures were in the process of rapid increase at the time this was written. A report at the writer's elbow states that at this moment the Axis nations probably hold more than fifty per cent of the world's coal and iron ore. Their control of oil has certainly risen well above the figures given here, and they are reported now to possess more manganese than the United Nations.

The wealthy are always loath to believe that they can ever be poor. They cannot see the approach of the clammy hand of adversity until it is actually upon them. The Russians of the Tsar did not know that their power had disappeared until the ground had actually crumbled beneath their feet. The French aristocrats danced disdainful of the glowering mob though the sources of their pomp and position had already been eroded past all recognition. The control exercised by the United Powers over the native resources and riches of the earth is fading into pale theory. Only a specious legality makes it true today before the established fact of Axis possession.

If the Axis powers can succeed in their appointed task to quarantine America from the rest of the world, long enough to enable them to establish control over the great Eurasian-African-Oceanic land mass, our dream of outbuilding them on land, sea or air will become a fantasy. Even under the hypothesis that we had taken control of Central and South America and were able to exploit their manpower and resources with the same thoroughness and authority which the Axis would employ over its subjects, we would have under our control a population of 274,110,000. This would compare with that under Axis domination of 1,870,770,000.

This endless mass of regimented humans would be

promptly put to work at tasks which serve the continuously mushrooming Axis military machine. In industrial capacity, as well as in vital raw materials, we should soon find ourselves outstripped in every direction. Every vaunted superiority of arsenal, mill and factory on which we now rely for eventual victory, would tragically disappear. We would then be on the defensive—not because we willed it so—but because there would be no help for it.

The full measure of the gigantic accomplishment toward which Axis policy is relentlessly driving and which would be the final step in preparation for the coup in force against proud, insolent, and rich America, may be had from tables of comparative resources:

North and South America have together only 38.3% of the total world pig iron output. The entire Western Hemisphere produces only 37% of the world's bauxite. It is responsible for only 8.22% of the total chrome, 7% of manganese, .002% of tin, 44.45% of zinc, 31% of iron, 45.8% of lead, 33% of mercury, 14% of magnesium, 43.8% of petroleum, 1.9% of rubber, 30% of wool, .0007% of silk, 27.9% of coal, and 4% of synthetic rubber.[10]

In waterpower resources North America possesses 27,000,000 horses with a potential of 115,000,000. This almost equally matches the existing horses in waterpower resources of Europe. The potential, however, of the Eurasian-African land mass is 390,000,000 horses.[11]

[10] On the other hand it produces sixty per cent of the world's copper, seventy-five per cent of vanadium, and eighty-seven per cent of nickel.

[11] Nels A. Bengtson and Willem van Royen, *Fundamentals of Economic Geography;* Walter H. Voskuil, *Minerals in Modern Industry;* A. Roush, *Mineral Industry.*

Based on the most recent figures available, production and industry for the Americas is not more than twenty-seven per cent of the world's total, leaving the competing Eurasian-African aggregate with seventy-three per cent.

Even then, many of the critical materials which remained to us would have to be hauled over considerable distances by water and would be subject to incessant harassment by submarines, aircraft, and surface raiders. All of our nitrates, practically all of our tin, and a good share of our copper would have to be transported over the long water route from harbors on the Chilean coast along lines of communication which would be hazardous, if not doubtful altogether. Practically all of our chrome would have to be carried from below the Equator. We would rely on Brazil, Bolivia, and the Argentine for a great portion of our tungsten ore, and for an important part of our rubber, wool, silk, and bauxite.

The final act in this gruesome drama would be a spectacular invasion by air and sea against South America. Native Fascists and Axis agents would prepare the ground and attempt the *coups d'état* which would wreck resistance in advance and render the vast domain easy prey. From here an effort would be made to outflank the Panama Canal and our own southeastern coast by storming the Caribbean Islands in a series of aerial troop movements similar to that at Crete.

Another type of envelopment, which is on the alternate chart of the Axis leaders, would be to take the United States directly from the north by a lateral turn-

ing operation. Hawaii would be bypassed after a feinting attack directed at Lower California, in which the
Japanese would write off substantial losses as a necessary investment. Behind this screen the real assault
would be delivered against Alaska, with an air-borne
army of half a million men swooping down and occupying the valleys in the defender's rear. If Alaska could
be taken by the Japanese, it could be securely held by
them. The presence of an immense, untraversable wilderness on the land side practically makes the big peninsula a distant island, more accessible to the eastern
shore of Siberia than to the United States.

The fall of Alaska would make an invasion of our
West Coast inevitable; and had the balance of the
Axis timetable operated smoothly and without hitch,
the preponderance of force which could be brought to
bear against us would be prodigious. The whole action
would be one of swift precision movement, with more
than a million men brought in on wings in a matter
of days. The first incursion would seek to tear away
the West Coast in a great slash of shark's teeth, and
here, too, military logic would assume an ability to
retain possession. Once the coastal fringe had been acquired, the Rocky Mountains with the great desert and
wilderness areas lying to their rear, form a perfect
cushion against counter-attack.

Synchronizing itself as the opposite wing of this
huge envelopment, the Wehrmacht would come in,
also on wings, in a monster air-borne procession following along two major tracks. One would reach up
from the roof of the South American bulge, hopping
along the islands of the Caribbean. The other would

leap from Britain to Iceland to Greenland, from there spreading in two secondary prongs to our East Coast and Middle West, an insatiable horde, the product of an industrial capacity, fanaticism and will to victory far outmatching ours.

This is the great megalomaniac project which is implicit in the Axis blueprint. It must be taken seriously. In innumerable military tomes, in the carefully worked out designs of Professor Haushofer's Geo-political Institute in Berlin, in the violent jargon of a myriad of Nazi *gauleiters*, big and little, and in the ponderous mass of military and technical literature of Germany and Japan, this ambitious plan is written. No power but that of irretrievable defeat will halt these men whose mission is slavery and whose ideal of human culture is iron-handed Caesarism. The fantastic concepts which wrap this vision in a maze of improbability do not rob it of its ever-present dangers. The men who organized and instituted it could not stop it now if they wished. It has become a way of life for whole nations, an expression of their mission on this earth, which can only end in total victory or utter defeat.

The only question which exists is whether the Axis is equal to the Gargantuan task it has set for itself. The timetable miscalculated twice—once when the military masters of Berlin misjudged the character of the British people and the resources of combative spirit and fighting machines which remained at their disposal when all hope seemed gone. The second error was a complete misjudgment of the strength and physical position of the Russians. Just as they misunderstood the fortress power of a modern island surrounded by a wall of hard-fighting airplanes, they overrated the pre-potency of their familiar blitz tactics when transferred to the conditions of Russian geography. In particular, they erred in their judgment of Russian psychology, believing that the U.S.S.R. would fold up like a balloon once it had been successfully entered.

It would be misleading to believe that these failures will deter men who, in their march to power, declared, "We will either rule or tear the world down in flames with us." [12] One thing is certain: Nothing will dissuade the Germans from attempting to adhere rigidly to their own time schedules. If they win they become the ruling masters of the world, fulfilling the passionate German dream of centuries. If they lose they will be a Pariah people, wildly hated by a Europe they have ruined and brutalized, and which sits sullenly by waiting for the day of revenge.[13]

As this is written the German war machine has been held up for more than a year by unexpected Russian stubbornness, by military miscalculations, and by the icy weapons of that ancient ally of the Slavs, the bitter Russian winter.

As the warmth of early summer dries the morass of sticky clay roads and loosens the congealed oil which has held the German motors imprisoned, the *Wehr-*

[12] Statement by S.S. Chief, Captain Roehm, before the Nazi accession to power.

[13] This is a situation which will not be allayed in the slightest by the wordy assurances of diplomats and politicians, or the issuance of a new set of "Fourteen Points."

macht will concentrate all its desperate, stored-up power in the Southern theater. The armies of Rommel's *Afrika Korps* will peck viciously away at the British imperials defending the Nile. The principal engagement will be a powerful smash against the lower anchor of the Russian line, in an attempt to pour through the Caucasus into the relatively unprotected Near and Middle East.

Contact would then be made with the Japanese, who will be expected to push up a thin column from India. The great British Empire which had been the dominating factor of six generations of global strategy, would then have been smashed into fragments like a crushed walnut. China would be cut off from the outside world and gradually suffocated. The Soviet Union would find itself largely isolated and would be compelled to fight on an enormously elongated front, subjecting its important industrial areas in Asia and the Urals to smashing attacks from its exposed rear.

Hitler's road through the Caucasus is blocked, however, by a powerful Russian Army and a difficult mountain region requiring the forcing of narrow passes. If this leg of the journey could be successfully completed, the *Fuehrer's* armies would be confronted with the thousand-mile wilderness which borders on Baluchistan, or would be compelled to take the almost impassable road through Afghanistan to the Khyber Pass and thence through the Himalayas.

This would not be an easy enterprise to complete— but neither was that of Hannibal when he brought his Ibero-Numidians and their elephants across the Alps to Italy. And it would pay rich dividends by bringing the Axis partners finally within actual sight of victory.

No one knows exactly how strong the Soviets are or how weakened they have been by the death of their sovereign ally, winter. It is expected that the Germans will make a competent adjustment to the new type of conditions they found involved in war on the steppes. But actually our estimates are all arrived at by surmise and guess. Despite the factual alliance which ties our destiny to the success of their arms, we know almost nothing about the Russians—their troop dispositions, their installations, or their output of ordnance, munitions, planes, tanks and other machines of war. One is tempted to say that we know even less about our Russian co-fighters than we do of the Nazi enemy.

By a careful examination of the events which have preceded we may safely assume that the morale of the Russians is unimpaired and that they do not lack the will to continue this contest to the end. Their armies are apparently in good shape, well disciplined, numerous and confident, though a doubtful match for the superbly organized *Wehrmacht*. The destruction of the great factory belts and centers of hydro-electric power east of Moscow no longer looms over the military picture as the disastrous circumstance it first appeared to be.

The Soviets have created within a few years what seems to be a full-size industrial development hidden in the Ural Mountains, a good thousand miles back of the lines. Here are reputed to be inexhaustible resources of coal and most of the other raw materials required in the manufacture of war goods. There is oil from which high octane gasoline may be derived, as well as iron, salt, potash, copper, zinc, asbestos, nickel, and bauxite. In this area are great power plants linked in an interchangeable network served by railroads and motor roads. The city of Magnitogorsk is one of the great industrial complexes of the world, the red flames of its foundries belching forth day and night. In this zone are said to be gigantic tractor plants, machine-tool shops and factories and yards turning out rolling stock, airplanes, engines, submarines, electrical equipment and ordnance of all kinds.

Lease-Lend goods from America, as well as a stream of supplies from Britain, are being delivered to Stalin through the Persian Gulf, and thence overland to ports and railheads on the Caspian Sea, or are flown directly to the Soviets from delivery points in Iran. Other material flows along the North Atlantic route to Archangel, and during the summer months, down the Northeast Passage stretching from the Seward Peninsula in Alaska through the Arctic Ocean to Murmansk and Archangel.

If the Russians are passably well supplied with airplanes, tanks and munitions, the superiority of their position will be dictated by their own vast spaces and the inexhaustible man-strength at the disposal of their commanders.

While our assistance has by no means been of decisive importance it has added materially to the strength of Russia's winter offensive against the invader. The British have sent approximately 1200 Hurricanes and Spitfires and the United States almost 2000 fighters of the Airacobra, P-40, and P-35 types. If we were able to place in Russia during the next six months, 5000 heavy bombers and modern pursuit jobs with their equipment and personnel, together with a force of half a million men on caterpillar treads, the quick winning of the war would be a foregone conclusion. We would then be able to reverse the situation which spears us on the points of the Axis circumference, operating on sound interior lines rather than on the periphery as at present. However, the questions of transport and supply, as well as of training and manufacture, place the implementation of such a plan beyond any means now at our disposal.

In Asia the eastern forces of the Soviet probably total over half a million well-trained and equipped men. Facing them are some 400,000 Japanese, about 350,000 in Manchukuo and 150,000 in Korea, but the little brown men could probably mass a million warriors in this area in quick order if required.

The great weakness of the Russian position is the fact that it almost outflanks itself. It is dependent for all transport on the Trans-Siberian Railroad which runs for 1000 miles along the flat plains near the border of Manchukuo, and which could be severed by any determined incursion.[14] The one circumstance which would deter the Japanese from this adventure is the existence of a great air base at Vladivostok, within short bombing range of the big industrial cities of Japan and only 680 miles from Tokio itself. Any at-

[14] Another parallel railway is being double-tracked several hundred miles to the north of the present line, but even this, when completed, will lack the protection of strategic barriers.

tempt to wrench Siberia from the Russian grasp would cost the Nipponese dearly unless it were accompanied by a successful lightning assault against the port of Vladivostok.

The admirable vigor displayed by the Russians in resisting the might of the German steamroller has far exceeded the most hopeful expectations. Russia, nevertheless, must be considered a great question point on the map of relative resources. Her overall situation depends entirely on what the Anglo-Saxon powers are able to do in the West. If we are following any policy which does not involve a direct attack on the German Reich this summer, we will have to write Russia off our list of assets before another year rolls around. The Muscovites cannot win the war for us alone.

Another great question mark is China. The strength and staying power of the great Oriental colossus must be reappraised in view of our present knowledge of the fighting qualities of Japanese armies. For years the Chinese military force, which had always been regarded as a paper army by the Western powers, has been able to keep the great murderous Japanese instrument of blitzkrieg locked in a deadly struggle for possession. The Chinese have steadily retreated and have, of course, been aided by their magnificent sweeps of country. Though beaten back, their armies are still intact and confront the enemy along 3800 miles of battleline, more resolute than ever.

Like the Russians who moved whole industries to the Urals, the Chinese have taken with them the machinery of many hundreds of the most modern industrial plants of eastern China in their withdrawal

westward. Seventy thousand machines were transported across mountains and rivers under constant
aerial attack, to re-create machine shops, foundries,
metallurgical, chemical and electrical works, and other
manufactories. Since the war began almost 2000 new
factories were opened in eleven industrial centers alone.
China's diversified steel mills, while small, are turning
out considerable quantities of metal and her infant
industry is making growing amounts of armament and
heavy stuff of all kinds.

The ingenuity and stamina shown by this great people should not be underrated. They are busy as ants
improvising new truck routes to replace the shattered
Burma Road, and there is a vast highway construction
program taking place in the far West, with connecting
arteries planned to India via Assam, Burma and Tibet,
and through the northwest into Siberia, there to link
up with Russian rail communications at Alma Ata and
thence to the Persian Gulf and the Mediterranean.
The route is circuitous and difficult, but represents an
undeniable and effective contact with the producing
West.

The leader of the Kuomintang, the Generalissimo
Chiang Kai-shek, probably has 3,000,000 soldiers under
arms. Were he able to equip them, he could undoubtedly put 7,000,000 more into the field without trouble.
Possession of the necessary armament would enable
him to remedy a serious weakness in his own situation.
No strong central force yet exists in China to regu-
late the columns which pay allegiance to the semi-
independent warlords and powerful Mandarins. The
control of the Kuomintang over the powerful Com-

munist armies of Mao Tse-tung, and the so-called Kwangsi generals, Chung-hsi and Li Tsung-yen, is only a nominal one, while that over the great body of guerrilla fighters hardly exists at all. If the Generalissimo possessed adequate arms, he would have the prestige and authority to cement all these diverse elements into one co-ordinated fighting unit.

The potentialities of China both as a military base and as an intrinsic fighting factor in this war, are incalculable. Together with the great sub-continent of India this sprawling territorial mass splits the Axis in two like a gigantic wedge. If it could be used as the heart of our operations, it would immediately allow us to operate from the vantage of interior position, stealing the initiative away from the Axis by forcing it on the periphery. If a way could be found to supply the Chinese with large guns, tanks, and a sizable air force, this country would become a wicked pile driver in the United Nations' hands, which would crush the Japanese like so many eggshells. This would involve major difficulties of transport and a long job of preparation in which the time element is not in our favor.

Although the Chinese struggle has been notably gallant and heroic, Japanese occupation of India would gravely alter the situation both psychologically and physically. The Chinese have proven their capacity to resist. But they are also realists. The leaky conduit which now connects them to a free world and from which they draw both hope and a stream of badly needed supplies, would be bitten off. All air vents which made the process of suffocation endurable, would be relentlessly closed one by one. An astute and cunning Japanese policy based on the program of *Asia for the Asiatics*, abetted by the electrifying spectacle of the white man in full retreat from the plateaus and valleys of Asia, would reconcile the Chinese people to the new order.

The pivot to the whole Asiatic structure is India and the Near East. If the Near East goes, India goes with it. Thus it is entirely possible, if this struggle is to be fought under the terms of linear warfare which have so far dominated it, that the Near and Middle East will be the final battlegrounds, as they have been of many historic contests in the past.

The destruction of Malta, strongest British naval-aerial base in the Mediterranean, must be looked on as a distinct possibility. The Mediterranean, now shrunk to the size of an inland lake by virtue of air power, may become untenable to the British Fleet. If Haifa and Malta can be obliterated, there is nothing to hinder the continued transfer of war material and men to North Africa for a full-dress assault on Egypt coincident with the attack through Turkey and the Caucasus.

What Turkey would do in this event may not be stated with certainty. The mere fact that she did not elect to uphold her part of the mutual assistance pact with Greece when the Italians debouched down on that little country, speaks volumes for the sagacious respect the Turks hold for the German military machine. However, the question is not of grave import since Turkey has little with which to oppose a German aggression whether she willed to do so or not.[15]

The abutting Arab states have no military strength or resistance power. The Arab looks picturesque and ferocious on his camel but is no match for modern instruments of war or the men who wield them.[16] When the pro-Axis leader, Rashid Ali el Gailani, seized authority in Iraq a mere handful of British Imperials overthrew him and forced the capitulation of the Iraqian Army.

Throughout the Arab world an unappeasable pro-Hitler rage has existed for years. In most of Arabia a Christian cannot even set foot under penalty of death. Yemen is tied up with Italy. The other Arab states are held by force or purchase and are completely unreliable.

A trained army of 250,000 loyal men fighting on familiar territory could make a world of difference at this moment of the war. When the present war began, several hundred thousand young Jews of Palestine, many of them European-trained as soldiers and officers, volunteered to fight for Britain and her allies. They are still waiting to be called. They know the desert and how to fight in it, and have a willingness to fight Fascism unmatched anywhere in the world, since they know what will happen to them and

[15] Even today the Germans are able to transfer troops and matériel from Western Europe to Libya within two or three weeks. It takes the British two or three months to ship men and supplies around the Cape to the Middle East.

[16] The military strength of the Arab states is as follows: Iraq, 19,000; Egypt, 32,500; Saudi Arabia, 2000. In each of these countries there are also a certain number of irregulars operating as a coast guard or border patrol.

their families should Germany prevail in the Middle East.

British policy in this sector, acquiesced in by the American State Department, is one of yielding to blackmail by a potential enemy. Declaring that "a Jewish army of 200,000 men would make the defenses of the Suez Canal almost impregnable," Congressman Andrew L. Somers roared to his peers: "First we saw Munich, then we saw appeasement in the Far East, and then we saw appeasement in the Near East. Today, Munich is past, today Japanese appeasement is past, yet appeasement is still in force in the Near East."

The explanation offered from British official quarters is that the Arabs will not enlist and they do not wish to offend them by allowing the Jews to do so.

The attitude of the 390,000,000 people of India toward this war is a mixture of irascibility, hope, indifference, and apathy. Mohammedans dislike Hindus and both combine to resent the presence of their European overlords. Pro-Asiatic slogans have a considerable audience, and the usual quota of ambitious young politicos are in direct contact with the Axis.

India will be difficult to defend,[17] although the terrain is not favorable to the invading side. Great areas of mountain and swamp intervene between the two

[17] The Japanese have a complete index on everything in India. They were an important part of the social life there and ran a regular service of steamers between the Hooghly River and Japan. "It may be taken for granted," says Sir Alfred Watson, "that everything that the Japanese military chiefs might desire to know about India and its approaches is duly indexed in Tokio and the possible Quislings among the Indians will all be scheduled." (*Great Britain and the East*, January 3, 1942.)

borders and there are few roads. If attacked simultaneously from East and West, the fall of the great sub-continent would seem to be inevitable and would invite with it the collapse of all Asia.

The position of Rommel's *Afrika Korps*, the nether end of the pincers aiming at Suez and the Near East, depends altogether on how much strength the United Nations can throw into this sector. Rommel's mere existence is a mounting danger to the already precarious Allied position. Only the concentration of overwhelming force will drive him out, and this is not in sight.

Rommel's rear is commanded by French North Africa. Vichy is accused of having aided him with equipment, transport, and supplies. This ideological satellite of the Rome-Berlin-Tokio alliance may be presumed to occupy the identical state of non-belligerency once tenanted so successfully by Italy and now by Spain.[18] Instead of loyally supporting the Free French under de Gaulle, the American Government still elects to placate the sinister Fascist hierarchy which now rules unhappy France.

The position in reference to Spain is just as difficult to understand. The little rotund *Caudillo* is the principal instrument of the violently anti-Yankee propaganda with which the Axis attempts to agitate South

[18] In Washington, London, and Cairo are still the French and Spanish Embassies, representing governments which are owned body and soul by America's number one enemy. There is also the Finnish Legation representing a country whose whole future is tied up with the victory of Germany. These elements are in a splendid position to connive, to observe information of a military nature which cannot be hidden from their gaze, and to transmit this intelligence by protected diplomatic pouch.

America. He has never expressed any other view than that of complete solidarity with the poisonous ruffians who rule the strongholds of Berlin, Rome, and Tokio. Not only do we allow this alleged neutral to fracture the embargo we are attempting to maintain against Nazi Europe, but we also supply him with goods imperatively needed by ourselves. British money interests are alleged to have furnished him with mining machinery—some of which may be Lend-Lease—despite the fact that none of the United Nations can obtain enough machinery to use for their own required war production. This equipment goes to the famous Rio Tinto Mines, one of the world's most important copper sources. It may be suspected that the greatest portion of their output eventually finds its way into Axis shells and other armament.

Portugal, ostensibly allied with England, has been under a Fascist-type dictatorship for a generation. When the writer was in Lisbon last winter it was full of Italian and German officers with whom the Portuguese military men fraternized openly. Portugal should be completely discounted in appraising our stock of assets. In any event, its combatant power is slight, and the country could be taken overnight by a land invasion.

Once all supplies are cut off from Spain,[19] that state may be expected to join the Axis openly and, with it, Portugal. On the other end of the Mediterranean,

[19] The report of Archibald MacLeish, Chief of the Office of Facts and Figures, on March 11, 1942, accuses the Japanese Embassy in Madrid of being a clearing house for Axis propaganda against the U.S.A.

Egypt despite the presence of belligerent British troops is technically neutral, and does not matter much anyway.

The only military factor of any consequence on the balance of the African continent is the Union of South Africa. Here there is serious question as to the loyalty of the Boer minority. Nazism has made considerable progress among these people, and with it a substantially developed fifth column. A typical outcropping is the motion introduced in Parliament by General Hertzog, leader of the Nationalist Boer Opposition, demanding "immediate termination" of the state of war with Germany into which South Africa "against her will and best interests" has been "dragged" by "the Imperial connection." Comments van Paassen acidly: "The motion was defeated by a significantly small majority." [20] If the Germans should ever be able to penetrate to the border of this commonwealth, the South African Union will be found to be a house divided against itself and will fall like an overripe plum.

There is little to take comfort from in this situation, and the South Pacific theater is even more unsatisfactory. Here we have made the sorry mistake of heavily discounting the Japanese who are a truly great military nation, capable of every exercise of strategy, power and organization which has distinguished the great white empires of this century. They are brave, ingenious, resourceful, numerous and far-seeing and the state which beats them will know that it has been in a brawl of first class dimensions. The Battle of Gran

[20] *The Time is Now*, p. 47.

where the Mongol, Sabutai, destroyed the combined armies of Europe shatters any illusion that it is only the white race which can furnish great military captains. Says Mitchell prophetically: "Asia produced these wonderful generals; and it may produce similar generals in the future." [21]

The Japanese have fanned out over an enormous territory split into a thousand fractions separated by great gaps of water. There is not a single province which they have yet succeeded in reducing to order and submission. They are strung out over thousands of miles of thinly held lines of communication. This is the great Japanese weakness. Their strength lies in the enormous capacity for social organization which characterizes this people, and which has enabled them to leap from a feudal style economy to a full-blown, modern industrial competitor in the space of a generation. It may be reliably expected that Nippon will quickly organize the resources of the areas it has captured and that these will be strongly held against any counterattack, with every factor of position and armed strength favoring the possessors.

Except for the sentimental reason of being a sister English-speaking nation, Australia possesses no direct or critical relationship to the outcome of the war. The stepping-stone type of attack so often proposed, need not invite any great apprehension on the part of the Japanese warlords, whose vast industrial structure and well-organized communications give them an immense advantage over anything the United Nations are apt

[21] *Outlines of the World's Military History,* p. 241.

to improvise in Australasia. The Japanese can actually meet the United Nations on equal terms on the northern coast of the big island, and could, without doubt, seize Port Darwin and its adjacent fringe of shore and manage to hold on indefinitely.[22]

Eighty-five per cent of Australia's 7,000,000 people live in and around the cities of the southeast, and here her industry is located. It is most unlikely that Japanese naval vessels will be able to approach this stretch of coast as long as it is defended by a reasonably strong concentration of aircraft. To have even a fighting chance for success, the Japanese would have to leave their principal islands unguarded by moving their entire fleet into the south and staking it all on a desperate gamble in Australia. This would amount to an engraved invitation to the Russians in Vladivostok and East Siberia to move down on Manchukuo and to send their squadrons shuttling over Tokio, Osaka and Yokohama. This is far too hazardous a venture for the hard-headed Japanese, who would see little enough to gain by it.

The only other direction of attack against Australia would be over the northern and western stretch of desert. This forbidding waste, the home of a few rem-

[22] The Japs probably maintain around 1,000,000 men on their own islands. Another 100,000 must be stationed at outlying bases. The East Indies absorb another 400,000, and an equal number are on the Burma front. Siam and Indo-China probably hold about 100,000. A half million men or more must be located in Korea and Manchukuo and there should be in the neighborhood of 750,000 on the Chinese front. No one knows exactly what reserves Japan has left for the purpose of additional military adventure. So far there is no evidence of any real strain on her resources of manpower or war production.

nants of the wild aboriginal tribes, runs on for thousands of miles without water or roads. It lacks every consideration necessary to sustain large armies, which would have to bring with them all water, foodstuffs, goods and shelter they would require.

Despite its small population, the conquest of this country would involve a first class military effort and the Japanese presumably know this better than anyone. For the first time they would encounter a well-industrialized, tough and modern people, whose factory centers are a beehive of industrial activity. Australia now turns out several hundred fighting planes a month, and so many anti-aircraft guns that she is actually exporting them. She manufactures small arms, bombs, textiles, field guns, tanks, armor plate, optical glass, and war material of every description. The commonwealth has seven shipyards building destroyers and small naval vessels. At a single plant at Broken Hill 1,000,000 tons of steel are produced annually.

The whole question of Australia's defense hinges around air power, of which she certainly possesses more than can be brought against her from a distance. A spectacular overnight assault would appear to have very little hope of success and the Dominion should be able to defend itself for a period equal to the time the Japanese are actively engaged elsewhere. If she is beaten it will be because most of the machine tools and raw materials used in her war factories have to be imported, subjecting her to the dangers of blockade.

As an offensive base Australia simply does not add up. It does not produce enough to equip a great invading army. Everything from men and guns to food and materials would have to run the long gantlet across the Pacific. From Port Darwin to the Panama Canal is 8192 miles. It is 3300 miles to Honolulu. These are indeed perilous lines on which to base an offensive, which could, moreover, on no count, have any decisive bearing on the outcome of this war.

Despite the assurances of good-will which have resulted from Pan-American conferences, the big pear-shaped continent to which we are tied by the Isthmus of Panama could easily turn out to be our true heel of Achilles.

A number of the Latin countries are ruled by dictators directly, men who are fascinated by the naked credo of power and impressed by armed strength. Many of the Latin-American military forces were German trained and are open admirers of Nazi "efficiency," though pro-American influence is on the rise. There are extensive German and Italian population blocs, plus a considerable number of Japanese, groups which are influential far beyond their numbers.

The Axis has played cleverly upon the cupidity of the great commercial shoguns and plantation owners, pointing out to them tirelessly that the only logical market on this earth for their grain, beef, leather and other products is crowded, hungry Europe. The United States is shown to have normally a surplus of these same commodities and is painted, not without warrant, as an open competitor for such world markets as may exist. The traditional suspicion of the South American toward his *Yanqui* neighbor of the

North has lost none of its virility. An additional and recent phenomenon is the Pan-Spanish movement linking these peoples with their mother state in the Iberian Peninsula and indirectly with Italy and Germany.

Another point of friction lies in the fact that Argentina, for example, has imported from beyond this hemisphere over forty per cent of her iron and steel, seventy-five per cent of her coal and two-thirds of her copper needs, not to mention such commodities as dyes and chemicals. Chile has been dependent on overseas sources for nearly half her imports. The same is true of Brazil. These states now seek to buy from the United States products like iron bars, locomotives, coal and dyes which our embargo against the Axis prevents them from obtaining from Europe. To these realistic people it seems simple that while we may promise much, we are hardly in a position to deliver. "It is clear," concedes Vice-President Wallace, "that in supplying the minimum requirements of our Latin American neighbors and those of our war industries at home, the economic resources of the Western Hemisphere will be strained to the limit." [23]

We are seeking to buy our way into South America and sending them a tremendous flood of Lend-Lease dollars, in addition to the promise of guns and other supplies. As our position becomes more difficult the complete irrationality of this procedure will serve to halt it altogether. *The fact is that South America should be supplying us as a partner in this war, and*

[23] "Economic Basis of Inter-American Relations," *Free World*, March, 1942.

not the other way around. There is no limit to the
potentialities of the southern continent if it wishes to
enter this war in earnest and make the necessary sacri-
fices in the common cause. These countries "possess in
their soil," says J. Alvarez Del Vayo, "all the necessary elements for war industry. Mobilized within the
frame of a plan of co-ordinated economy they can
themselves provide the necessary supplies for the largest armies." [24]

An example of the general attitude is the great
boom the war has made in basic metals and nitrates
in Chile. She is now engaged in a profitable trade with
the United States and wishes to avoid all risk. Yet in
the name of some factitious good will we are expected
to supply her with railroad equipment, arms, and
planes desperately needed by ourselves.

Despite the warm friendship which Brazil displays
toward this country, it is plain that she does not contemplate joining the United Nations as an equal partner in risk and in expenditures. At the most she will
act against the Axis sub-sea fleet, to protect her shipping.

With Peru, we are even more open-handed in an
effort to offset Axis influence. Our Government has
purchased Peru's 400,000-bale cotton crop for $44,-
000,000, and will store it in Peru (presumably paying
storage costs) for the duration. Similar action, it is
said, will be taken on each crop until the end of the
War; and it is expected that we will also buy and store
locally next year the Paraguayan cotton crop and the

[24] "The Potential Forces of the Democracies," *ibid.*

2,500,000-bale Brazilian crop. All of this will probably be thrown on the market at a time, during the post-war period, when we will presumably have great cotton surpluses of our own which will have to be plowed under.

On the face of it, this sort of thing is a form of appeasement. It is a sign of weakness, and will not entitle us to that respect and loyalty we so earnestly seek from our Latin neighbors.

This does not mean that there are not earnest and well-meaning people throughout this area who see eye to eye with us in the great ideological cause to which we are dedicated. It simply means that from the view of practical politics South America remains on the fence, a serious potential menace in case the world picture worsens and the Axis succeeds in its design of placing our continent under a state of siege. Much of grave import is indicated in the announcement by the Spanish Foreign Ministry of March 14, that it had signed a far-reaching financial and commercial accord with the Argentine for an exchange of goods valued at half a billion pesetas, and calling for an eventual airline to link Madrid with Buenos Aires.

All of this wheat, beef, leather, and other products will be consistently siphoned into Germany and Italy. This is a concession which our government should find some method of voiding. In particular, a scheme to link Spain and the New World by air should be looked at askance. The source of this plan is without question Germany, who with Italy would be compelled to supply both planes and pilots for this run. Such an artery would be a continuation of the old Nazi-Italian network of airlines which served as a practical training ground for a future air invasion of the Americas.

The real extent of this danger is not comprehended by Americans. "If Germany flew one thousand bombers' to Brazil," observed an American airman, "and landed them on airdromes prepared by the millions of Germans now resident there, supplying through the air the necessary bombs and fuel, it would be necessary for the nation which would enforce Western Hemisphere defense to drive these bombers out." [25] But no land- or water-borne army could approach Brazil under the sphere of influence of these thousand bombers until they had first been destroyed or driven out. We should then have to send down an air force with sufficient power and range to attempt the smashing of these bombers on their Brazilian bases. "The ensuing air engagement would largely determine the issue; certainly it would settle the first or the air phase. This is how easily an aggressive foreign power could test our doctrine of hemisphere defense." [26]

Warning is given by Hugo Fernandez-Artucio that a bloodless war is already being carried on by Hitler's army in Latin America against us, and that "it will develop into invasion and bloodshed for these republics should Hitlerized Germany become the master of a devastated Europe or of a large area of the sea." [27] It

[25] Arnold and Eaker, *Winged Warfare.*
[26] Ibid.
[27] *The Nazi Underground in South America.*

is perfectly clear that the geographical position of Latin America makes it the natural battlefield for any action against the United States, unless energetic measures to protect their sovereignties are undertaken by the countries involved.

There are 2,000,000 Germans or Brazilians of German descent in the big Portuguese-speaking republic, a great portion of whom are attracted by Nazi doctrines. The Axis is reputed to spend $2,500,000 a month on propaganda alone. Near São Paulo a submarine base built for Axis raiders was discovered by police in a drive to liquidate a Japanese fifth column arm estimated at 25,000 men.[28] In Colombia, Japanese farmers have imported a large quantity of arms; in Peru they are secretly organized on a military basis.

The situation in the Argentine and Chile is already serious, and is based on the belief that the Axis will win the war. The Argentine is governed by the same commercial view which holds in Chile. It attempts to remain strictly "neutral," selling its beef and farm products for high prices, hoping to get machinery and manufactured products in exchange. A whole group of Argentine newspapers is definitely pro-Axis. A Congressional committee investigating anti-Argentine activity in 1941 reported that 60,000 German storm troopers were organized throughout the country under oath to serve Hitler to the death. Enormous sums are spent monthly in furthering the Nazi conspiracy

[28] In Brazil all subversive political activity has been outlawed and all foreign newspapers forbidden publication. The press, movies and radio are strictly censored. At least for the time being the Nazi situation seems well in hand there.

which seeks to achieve political and economic control by bloodless methods. The mass of the people is undoubtedly favorable to the United Nations, but despite some judicious pussyfooting the government veers over to the pro-Axis side. It does not hesitate to take summary action against pro-American newspapers when this suits its convenience.[29]

In Chile the situation is as unhealthy. It was recently reported by deputies in the National Congress that ninety-five per cent of the officers in the Chilean army were pro-German. It is claimed that every newspaper below Valparaiso is German controlled. When Hitler came to power in Germany "the swastika began to fly from all the German houses in such cities as Valdivia, Osorno, Temuco, and Puerto Montt . . . The High command of the Nazi party in Chile has its headquarters in the nation's capital, Santiago, where it directs all the activities of the German troopers and spies throughout Chile." [30] According to official estimates there are 35,000 members of the Nazi party, of whom 8000 have been organized under strict Nazi military discipline. These operate openly in their association with native Fascist leaders and with the Spanish Falangists and the Italian Fascist party. In connection is every kind of German organization—hospitals, *Hitlerjugend*, *Girl Scouts Alemanas*, and numerous Nazi propaganda societies. There is an underground apparatus for trained fifth-columnists, the *Deutsch*

[29] A case in point is the arbitrary suspension on April 7, 1941, of the anti-Axis newspaper, *La Hora*, for exposing Nazi control of the Buenos Aires police force and various Government departments.

[30] Hugo Fernandez-Artucio, p. 170, *Free World*, March, 1942.

Chilenischer Bund, and the *Associacion de Amigos de Alemania* which links together native Nazi sympathizers.

II

The entire Axis conception of war hinges on far-flung global and geo-political concepts. The technique was evolved by men who know how to strike quickly and with crushing force, and whose sense of timing and organization is perfect. These men are aware that the single disastrous element in the imposing power-structure they have reared is the continued existence of Great Britain, pointed like a pistol at the very heart of the German giant. As long as England exists as a forward base for the operations of the United States, the United Nations will enjoy a tactical superiority certain to collapse the entire German war effort with fierce, unmerciful blows after American technological science has succeeded in evolving the proper instruments and technique of action.

This prospect must turn the dreams of Hitler and his General Staff into a nightmare of apprehension. As the American war effort develops it becomes more and more certain that if the *Fuehrer* is able to make juncture with his Eastern ally in Asia, he will stake everything on an effort to invade England. This project is still very much in the German mind and has not been abandoned by them simply because it cannot be.

Hitler has made intensive preparations for the invasion of Britain and will try it at some moment when he believes surprise is likely to be effective. He has in his control a large number of self-propelled barges designed specifically for this purpose, and is said to be building a great number of sea-sleds on the towed glider principle.

The plan would be to have heavy guns and an umbrella of seaplanes create a safe channel for the crossing. These would be synchronized with the use of cargo planes to carry both equipment and men. Garsia figures that 1500 troop-carrying planes with a brace of gliders apiece making successive trips and suffering, say, a thirty per cent loss on each crossing, could bring in a total of 200,000 troops in five trips.[31]

When considered against the backdrop of England's present strength, such a move would appear suicidal, but the Germans have never lacked audacity or nerve. If their eastern flank were once cleared, they would be certain to concentrate on the problem. German invasion tactics would undoubtedly involve a two-pronged thrust. One would be aimed at the sister island of Eire in an effort to isolate Britain by crippling her sea communications.

The Irish have nothing with which to resist such an aggression. Their army is not more than 13,000 men. Their air force consists of a few Beau-fighters, three or four Hurricanes, a Hudson and a Wellington which cracked up in their territory and were promptly confiscated, a few German Heinkels which badly need repair and for which spare parts do not exist, and a handful of Ansons, Lysanders, and Gladiators. This little green isle possesses a strategic bearing which makes it the second most important pivot point in the war. The

[31] Lieut. Colonel Clive Garsia, *Planning the War.*

tactical situation has not changed since the time Napoleon remarked that "had I gone to Ireland instead of to Egypt, the British Empire would have found its end." [32] If Eire was in German hands the big Focke-Wulf planes which patrol the gray wastes of sea would have a field day. Very few merchant ships would succeed in running unscathed through this vertical cordon.

It would appear that the only sound military course open to Germany at the moment against Britain is blockade. Whether this were accomplished through control of the seas themselves, of the air over the seas, or through the medium of lurking undersea boats, is not important. If merchant shipping could be kept from entering Britain, the island would be starved into submission within a short period. More than 600 ships with a total gross tonnage of over 7,000,000, must be kept continuously at sea to bring in the annual minimum of 40,000,000 tons of food, cotton, rubber, lumber, oil, ores, machinery, and other vital supplies required to sustain British life and continue the scale of military resistance.

The Germans are known to be concentrating on the

[32] There is a certain amount of pro-German feeling in Ireland, particularly in the ranks of the Anglophobic Irish Republican Army. The writer spent some three hours with Mr. de Valera in November of 1941 and talked at length with other members of the Government, and is convinced that the thinking Irish as well as those in authority in the Free State, have a clear understanding of the issues in this war. The situation as it stands is not satisfactory. It leaves the Free State exposed and places our own war effort in jeopardy. Common sense negotiations which took cognizance of all the circumstances on both sides and bypassed the brittle vagaries of professional diplomacy, should find little difficulty in solving this obstinate and vexatious problem.

manufacture of great numbers of U-boats and to have gone through a carefully prolonged period in training their crews. The effectiveness of the submarine campaign in the last war was indicated by the admission of then Prime Minister Lloyd-George that at one time Britain was only "six weeks from starvation." If the Germans are building large fleets of air and undersea craft suitable to predatory action against cargo-carriers, the prospect is forbidding. When the reserves are sufficiently large the fleet will be suddenly sprung in a violent surprise action which will seek to drive Allied shipping off the seas in a single operation. The Nazis' present assault on Allied shipping may be regarded in the light of a probing operation to establish technique and proficiency, and to iron out the bugs in the whole pattern of tactics.

The U-boats now hunt in packs, subjecting their victims to cross-fire shelling. The German Admiralty has also experimented on attacking our sea-borne commerce directly off its ports of origin, before there has been time to make up convoys. Oil tankers have been the favorite victims, suggesting an attempt to break up any American aerial offensive at its source by destroying the oil on which it will depend.

The prescription for a successfully handled war is to prepare always for the worst—to overestimate the enemy rather than underestimate him. Losses due to sinkings are now serious but may become infinitely more so. The sea war has reached a critical stage and is placing increasingly widespread demands on our already burdened facilities. We are trying to maintain supplies to Russia, to send U. S. troops and matériel all over the world, to keep oil and other production flowing to Britain, to create a base in Australia, to assist China, and to keep the water lanes open everywhere. This is an almost impossible job of convoy alone and can only be handled if we are able to maintain unchallenged control of the seas.

Meanwhile our battle fleet, on which we must depend for these difficult duties, has been heavily weakened as a result of events in the Pacific. The navy of our British ally has suffered the same proportionate casualties.

The escape of the battleships *Scharnhorst* and *Gneisenau*, along with the heavy cruiser *Prinz Eugen*, means that the Germans now possess a substantial fleet which can operate out of the North Sea and actually challenge the British Navy for control of nearby waters.[33] This armada includes the battleship *Tirpitz*, the pocket battleships *Lützow* and *Admiral Scheer*, the aircraft carriers *Graf Zeppelin* and *Deutschland*, together with four heavy and eight light cruisers and about twenty-five destroyers. It is probable that the Nazis have already completed two battleships of the 45,000-ton class, the *Friedrich der Grosse* and *Hindenburg*. Such a striking force could be used with overwhelming effect against convoys. It could sever British lines to Archangel, and might conceivably raid Iceland.

The Italians can add to this total five battleships, thirteen cruisers and seventy destroyers. In the Pacific, the Japanese have nine battleships, 111 destroyers,

[33] Continuous aerial attacks on these battleships, tucked away in their new berths, are said to have damaged them so severely as to take them out of action until fall.

thirty-eight cruisers, and five aircraft carriers. The Russian news agency, Tass, reports from Cairo on March 8, that forty French warships being built at the time of the French armistice had been handed over by the Vichy Government to Germany. These included the 35,000-ton battleship *Clemenceau* and an 8000-ton cruiser, together with many submarines. This, if true, would constitute the first step of a general transfer of the French Navy to the Germans. The French fleet consists of five capital ships, about twenty-two cruisers, fifty-five destroyers, sixty submarines and a well-trained air arm which could be used in conjunction.[34] The addition to this powerful force to the Axis would make the Mediterranean untenable for the United Nations and might actually give the enemy almost ship for ship parity.

[34] Reagan (Tex) McCrary in *Daily Mirror*, Feb. 20, 1942.

V. DEFENSE OF THE AMERICAS

REALISTIC geo-military thinking dictates that we seize at once all land approaches to this continent, and that we establish an armed protectorate over all areas on our connecting continental land mass which might serve as springboards for an invasion of our shores.

Certainly no territory whose political reliability is doubtful and which enters into the strategical zone of our defense, should be permitted powers of external action which might seriously hamper that defense. To continue to do so at a time when we are engaged in a desperate battle for existence, is imprudent if not actually reckless. It is an expression of the same strained and lackadaisical mentality which has allowed the Axis to obtain the initiative and tactical superiority of position at every turn. The result was seen in the Battle of Norway, the invasion of the Low Countries, the assault at Pearl Harbor and in the absorption of Indo-China and Thailand. Only a state which is so inert and decrepit that it no longer possesses the energy to protect itself, would allow a condition of such potential menace to continue, when faced by such implacable and unscrupulous enemies as we and at so late and critical a stage in the game.

Under no circumstances should any anti-American piece of ground large enough to land an airplane on, be allowed to remain in foreign hands. In the Caribbean Sea, which Homer Lea refers to as "the second most important strategic sphere on the globe," [1] the West Indies and the Antilles completely dominate our Atlantic Seaboard and Gulf Coast as well as the indispensable Panama Canal and the entire littoral which runs down to the big bulge of eastern Brazil.

We should immediately lay hands on the French West Indies, which must be regarded as German outposts. There is reason to believe that German submarines have been operating from Martinique's harbor, the best in the Caribbean, and have been refueled there. The island lies about 370 miles from Puerto Rico and about 250 miles from South America. French Guadeloupe, consisting of two islands separated by a narrow strip of sea, is about 290 miles from Puerto Rico. There is a magnificent harbor at Pirate-a-Pitre and another in the Les Saintes group which strings out from the two main islands.

These places should be taken outright, and not merely immobilized by "agreement." Vichy's guarantees have not the slightest value and should be completely discounted. The protests of this puppet of Adolf Hitler can be quite sensibly ignored. Vichy sat inertly by when the British attacked the French fleet, and later swallowed Syria and Madagascar. The kidnapped areas can be held in escrow by us for an eventual return when the emergency is over. In fact, this hope dangled before Vichy's eyes would do more to keep her in line, if indeed she is a free agent, than all the appeasement efforts we can employ.

[1] *The Valor of Ignorance*, pp. 114, 115.

In the Pacific, the Galapagos should be a fully equipped United Nations outpost. On the far side of the Atlantic, the Azores, Cape Verde and Canary Islands are located like so many little sharp knives all facing directly on our lifeline. The Azores are an archipelago belonging to Portugal. They are almost ideally situated some 900 miles off the European coast, 1000 miles from the African mainland, and 1350 miles from Cape Race in Newfoundland. The Cape Verde group, also Portuguese property, are only 1550 miles from Pernambuco in the Western Hemisphere. The Canary Islands belong to Spain and are 2800 miles from Puerto Rico. It was proven in the spring of 1942 that secret bases for U-boats were maintained there, after American customs agents had interrogated the skipper of the Spanish freighter, the *Isla de Tenerife*.

We should not hesitate to seize these places, and with them Dakar, the most western point of the Old World and ideally situated for an attack on America. Its distance from Pernambuco, Brazil, is only 1715 miles. The naval harbor is large enough to hold the biggest ships afloat, and immediately east of the city is a plateau which can be made into a large modern airport. A mile seaward is the island fortress of Gorée, which rules the approaches to the harbor.

The Trans-Saharan Railroad is now rapidly being built to connect French West Africa with the Mediterranean, immensely enhancing its strategic importance and pointing it like a rifle directly at our vitals. A temporary line may be finished now, capable of taking troops and their armament from the Mediterranean to Dakar on short notice.

Airplanes operating from Dakar could raise literal hell with our shipping and would be within a few hours of the American continent. From its harbor an enemy navy would be closer to South American waters than we. This port is by far the strongest base in Africa. "The danger to the United States," says General Charles de Gaulle, "should Dakar fall into Nazi hands, is not somewhere in the future, but is imminent—immediate. It is only the lack of matériel which keeps Hitler from using French West Africa and that situation results only from his being temporarily unable to spare aircraft from the Eastern front."

If we acted to take this African citadel now, geographical considerations would allow us to hold it with a comparatively modest force. To the south is an impenetrable forest; in the north lies the Sahara Desert. The coastline is rocky and dangerous reefs make the approach from the Atlantic hazardous. Elementary air installations would make this natural fortress virtually impregnable.

It is also high time that we took cogent steps to place South America in a better relationship to this war. So far the Latin powers have placed very little at our disposal beyond good will, and for this we are granting in return a large portion of our precious industrial production.

We are short both the goods essential to Latin American needs and the ships to carry them, and it would be folly to give preference to Latin America over self-evident war needs. We should stop making these injudicious promises to Latin American businessmen and should condition them to the fact that there is a war going on, and that they are part of the Western Hemisphere, as well as of a stricken world civilization. This is a grim and dreadful test of strength, and South America as well as the English-speaking union to the north must put her men and resources to work to overcome the common enemy. To do less is to do nothing. She must engage all of her factories and the total resources of her economy as well as her existing navy, land, and air forces. She could easily manufacture bombers according to specifications laid down by a joint War Board, in addition to other armament, and could contribute tankers and ships as well as raw materials.

This is a military matter, not an economic one, and not one in which diplomacy is involved on the old terms. Diplomacy created this war and may cause us to lose it. This conflict will not be won by fine talk or by resolutions of moral purposes. It will only be won if all those who will be affected by its outcome get together with a will and a toughness of purpose equal to that of our Axis opponents.

We could make a convincing start psychologically were we to organize a Pan-American Legion composed entirely of volunteers from Latin America. This brigade equipped as a self-sufficient unit with the best we have in tanks and air support, should be incorporated as an ally within the framework of the regular United States armed forces. The participation of this unit would have a strong emotional and moral effect upon Latin America, which would soon learn to take pride in its exploits. Such a situation would cre-

ate a *de facto* entry into the conflict which need not
wait upon the pronouncement *de jure*.

II

If all the toll gates which secure the roads to our
continent—from the Azores, Britain and Iceland, to
Hawaii, the Galapagos and the Aleutians—are safely
held by us, our situation cannot become actually desperate, and a policy of defense may be sensibly considered. With all outposts securely in our possession
we are safe from anything but long-range surprise attacks of overwhelming power. We, on the other hand,
would have our battle stations right up against the
enemy's house so that we could practically see in his
windows. The element of proximity pyramids our attack powers, whereas those of our adversaries decrease
as the comparative distance increases. *We are in a position to assault his most fundamental installations;
he can only attack the armored bases on our circumference and can get at our vitals only with great cost
and difficulty.*

The present tendency is to discount all strategies of
defense on the theory that they have been outmoded
by some magic inherent in a modern war machine. It
is believed even by sober military men that the key
—the only key—to Hitler's astounding success was the
fact that he adopted an offensive strategy on a total
scale. This, of course, is as bizarre as the opposite
Chinese-Wall concept which once hypnotized these
same minds. Warfare is like any other viable thing on

this earth—it is subject to constant evolution as various stimuli are brought to bear on it. The advent of a new piece of ordnance, or a single revolutionary factor for which the enemy is unprepared, gives an appearance of marginal superiority to the aggressor which later experience in no sense warrants.

The defense is as essential and as potent today where instruments of position, will and equipment are equal, as it ever was. "Unless some element of surprise can be introduced into the offensive," remarks Captain Falls, "the odds are on its failure, except when the attacking army is so superior in strength or morale that the outcome is a foregone conclusion." [2] The *Royal United Service Institute Journal* [3] tells us that "the defense still holds an advantage over the offensive." The conventional units on caterpillar treads cannot pierce an elastic defensive line of great depth without power materially greater than that of the defender. Nor may he do so without the prospect of forbidding losses.

It is true that the character of defense has changed. It has taken on a complexion of mobility it lacked in the last European war. It is no longer passive; but it is nonsense to claim that because of this fact it has ceased to exist. The Battle of Britain itself was defensively fought and won. Tobruk fell in a single day in the summer of 1942 as the result of a powerful surprise air and tank attack. But this does not detract from the fact of the magnificent defense of this fortress in the earlier campaign of 1941, which speaks for

[2] *The Nature of Modern Warfare*, p. 94.
[3] November 1940.

itself. This bulwark which had stood between Rommel and the Suez Canal, and later became a springboard for the second Allied incursion against Libya, demonstrated the weakness of tanks when exposed to heavy converging gunfire. It made a clear case, too, for the fact that air attack on a concentrated object well screened by a curtain of anti-aircraft guns, loses the greatest part of its efficacy.

Additional proof was given in the defense of Malta and Corregidor. No other areas in the world have been so thoroughly blitzed, yard for yard. In Tobruk and Corregidor the besieger actually held that shining key to victory, air supremacy; nevertheless during the first siege Tobruk held out for eight months before the German-Italians were driven back, and Corregidor resisted for almost as long before it finally fell.[4]

The Battle of Midway was essentially a defensive operation, and so was the German campaign in Crete which was designed to hem in Turkey and keep British warships out of the Aegean. Another parrying action was the sweep of the slender column of British Imperials which swung out of Egypt to liquidate the pro-Nazi coup of Raschid Ali in Iraq.[5] This was also the case in the extension of that same campaign which reduced Syria, then threatening the British flank.

The fortress powers of great cities and their capacity to withstand siege has never been shown better than

[4] The answer is that neither of these spots presents a vulnerable surface. Each was intrinsically a perfect defense area handled by determined and skillful men. Neither offers a "rear" which may be paralyzed or occupied, nor nerve centers which may be knocked out at a blow.

[5] S. L. A. Marshall, *Armies on Wheels*, p. 35.

in the events which took place before Leningrad and Moscow. The entire resistance of Russia proves that the nations which had been overrun by Hitler were already set to collapse. They were like inflated skins which the German *Fuehrer* simply pricked, and were no longer in the true sense viable organisms.

Even the magnificent work of our navy in maintaining the present convoy system over virtually all the oceans of this globe, must be regarded primarily as a defensive activity.

Yet there are many weaknesses to the defense concept. It leaves much to fate, and if long continued is destructive to the collective morale and character. It has none of the attractions of a hard provocative encounter in which all is dared to win all. Unless it passes by rapid transition stages to the offensive, it can never offer the assurance of a complete liquidation of the challenge, and absolute decision.

It is not impossible, if circumstances forced us to this point, for America to adopt a strategy of total defense. By such a policy we might be able to resist indefinitely, until the menace directed against us had abated by reason of natural causes.

The only force which could possibly assume the responsibilities for this critical task is Air Power.

As long as we could hold our far-flung battle stations in both the Atlantic and the Pacific the advantage of both defense and attack would remain with us. No enemy could bypass these barricades with impunity. If we lost these areas but were able to retain the Aleutians and our bases in the Western Atlantic, the advantage of defense position would still remain with us.

The mustering of enemy offensive power against us would be entirely limited by space, since the ability of aircraft to develop full striking force decreases in proportion to the distance of their bases from the site of operations. With all outposts in our hands, the importance of this factor can hardly be exaggerated.

No matter what Axis resources may be eventually, productive facilities at the moment, as they relate to air power, overwhelmingly favor us. This potential capacity in both engines and frames is indicated by reference to the closely related motor car industry. In the United States there is one automobile to every four persons, whereas in the balance of the universe there is but one to every 155 persons. The world registration of all motor vehicles as of January 1, 1941,[6] was 45,376,891. Of this total the United States supplied 32,452,861. If to this is added Great Britain's 2,429,580 and Canada's 1,477,282, the rest of the world is left with only 10,252,306. These potentials are further illustrated by the fact that the United States produces in a single year 2,000,000 electric refrigerators, 1,000,000 vacuum cleaners and 1,500,000 washing machines, with the balance of the world's production adding to only a fraction of these figures. In a single twelve months we produced three times as much aviation gasoline as all Europe combined.

Were we to take complete advantage of the latent power these facts disclose, we could make our con-

[6] Including passenger cars, buses, trucks, Diesel units, etc.

tinent virtually invasion-proof. This would call for a radical readjustment of our entire concept of the nature of armed forces.

Our thinking would be in terms of an unlimited air force, one whose numbers were restricted only by the amount of raw material available and the factory capacity to turn them out. No basic material, power plant or floor space which could be useful in the manufacture of aircraft would then be devoted to any other purpose, except for those which related directly to the maintenance of the air fleet.

With the full energy and technological abilities of the nation concentrated on this single problem, our capacity to turn out fighting craft would spiral to fantastic proportions. We could think in terms of half a million planes of all descriptions, designed to take the maximum advantage of the defensive position.

Instead of constricting the air transport industry as we are now doing, we would have to follow an opposite course, vastly expanding it and making its use mandatory for all long distance travel, mail, perishables, and even certain heavy cargo. Exclusive cargo airports located with regard to dock, railway and highway facilities would become the hub of our domestic transport system.

The transportation bottleneck which now burdens our war effort would be broken. We would have at our disposal a magnificent network of interlocking airlane systems, allowing us to move materials and men swiftly from area to area.

The value of such tremendous mobility assumes grotesque proportions in terms of applied power. All the bombers, fighters and cargo carriers in the nation could be concentrated against a threatened sector within a matter of hours. Miami would be as near to Panama as it now is to Jacksonville, and Seattle could be as easily defended as Chicago.

From the economic side we would save impressive amounts of rubber, metals and other critical materials now consumed in the upkeep of small, slow linear vehicles, and there would be no roads or right-of-ways to maintain. When roadway costs are figured in, plus upkeep, gasoline and savings in mileage-time and depreciation charges, transportation rates on anything but the heaviest cargo would be appreciably lower than at present.

Transport planes are highly resistant to wear. There is no junking of them as in cars. The utility value of a modern airplane is hard to believe—it will fly 30,000,-000 ship miles per washout. A planned service integrated for maximum equipment utilization could conceivably get in the neighborhood of 3000 miles a day per plane, seven days a week.[7]

If such immense air power as we contemplate here were in existence, its defense strength would be incontestible. The only opponent it would need fear would be opposing air power of such prodigious fire volume, speed, and maneuverability as to literally drive the defenders out of the skies.

No surface operation attempted against us would have the vaguest chance of success. Even granting that

[7] Based on the performance of Boeing 307's or other comparable modern types.

our navy, by some unforeseen catastrophe, suddenly disappeared, a squadron of troopships attempting to cross the wilderness of ocean would find itself under devastating fire by swarms of big bombers and torpedo carriers before it was halfway to its target. "The attack," says Phillips, "would grow in intensity as the convoy approached. The invasion might not be stopped before it reached the coast but it would be badly damaged. Imagine then, this convoy attempting to come into a harbor and remaining practically stationary for days in narrow waters with the entire bombing force available to the U. S. working on it. The picture is incredible—the invasion would be doomed." [8]

Fixed defenses of any kind would be of little actual value. It would be a waste of money and effort to construct them, since they could be easily taken by a vertical envelopment or bypassed and outflanked.

Heavy expenditures in the way of anti-aircraft guns would be also, to a certain degree, open to question. We should not be misled by the ample curtain of protection anti-aircraft has given such places as Malta and Tobruk. The protection of a small natural stronghold against bombardment presents an entirely different problem than a large-scale effort to guard an extensive area. The latter, with its factories, power stations, munitions dumps and other sensitive zones, may be approached by surprise and can never hope to achieve the concentrated volume of protective fire given a strategic pinpoint of intrinsic fortress quality.

[8] Lieut. Colonel Thomas R. Phillips, *Army Ordnance*, Issue of September-October 1941.

By far the best protection against an irruption of hostile raiders is opposing airplanes. The reckless expenditures in ammunition and man-hours involved in the usual type of anti-aircraft work, makes the cost prohibitive in relation to the expected results.

The existence of high altitude bombers compels the creation of heavier anti-aircraft guns, greatly increasing the problems of defense. The Germans are now using 130 millimeter anti-aircraft guns with an effective range estimated to be almost 35,000 feet, and are said to have succeeded in hooking up ultra-short-wave radio-locators to anti-aircraft batteries so that the locators continuously and automatically direct the fire. But judging by subsequent exploits of the R.A.F., none of this has been of any great value. "To shoot at a bomber 20,000 feet high," comments the English expert, Pemberton-Billing, "is little more than a waste of time when it can be seen. When it is quite invisible the task loses all connection with logic or reason." [9]

Modern aircraft are tough and have again and again proven their ability to fly after being riddled with bullets, unless both pilot and second pilot are knocked out, the engines gone, or some essential portion of the craft literally blasted off. "Again and again," remarks Garnett, "British bombers have returned across the North Sea on one engine with pieces of the fuselage blown off, or even with pieces of the wing gone." [10]

On the subject of balloon barrages Pemberton-Billing observes caustically: "No definite figures have been given on this subject, but . . . if they were avail-

[9] Noel Pemberton-Billing, *Defense Against the Night Bomber.*
[10] David Garnett, *War in the Air*, p. 10.

able and could be divided into the total cost of putting up the barrage every night for all these months,
we would find that each bomber has probably cost
many millions of pounds to bring down." [11] In his
view, searchlights, too, have little value. They cannot
be focused on more than one raider. If there is a group
of invaders, they do little more than provide a confusing miscellany of information to the ground defenders. Moreover, they assist the enemy in locating the
target since the big lights will necessarily be around
the most important and exposed positions.

He considers that blackouts are equally useless, that
they make hysteria, destroy normal existence and hinder the use by defending pilots of airfields and other
facilities. The result is jangled nerves and a general
dislocation of traffic. Moreover, this stratagem does
not stop the enemy—it only stops the defending pursuits, who are unable to see the marauders clearly.
The incoming raider requires light, and actually drops
parachute flares in order to orient himself. The Germans have been experimenting with a method of light-
camouflage. At a signal of the alert a great blanket of
light is thrown over the endangered area by thousands
of beams flashing upward in a series of great cones.
This unique method is said to produce a blinding effect, completely blotting out the ground to the enemy
pilot.

It is not easy to determine where the facts lie in
this situation, but in a country of our dimensions the
whole scheme of anti-aircraft installation and the ef-

[11] *Defense Against the Night Bomber*, p. 50.

fort at blackout, would appear to warrant a careful re-examination.

As far as critical installations such as aircraft factories are concerned, the protection given by retaliatory ground fire is altogether insufficient. To place a fundamental reliance on this method, ignoring all other applying conditions, would be a piece of folly unequaled in this generation.

Without exception, all of our principal aircraft producing centers stand in an exposed position. Long-cruising submarines equipped with 16-inch guns could actually shell our West Coast plants. One can stand on the beach and almost look into the windows of these structures. Other undersea boats built to carry planes could rise to the surface before dawn, launch their craft and submerge without having been spotted. The great Douglas and North American aviation factories are within easy reach of raiders, as are those of Vultee, Consolidated and Boeing. On the East Coast the beautiful big Martin factory, whose loss would be coequal to a severe defeat on the field of battle, sits on an open field. Like other factories, attention is called directly to it by the shiny tops of thousands of workers' cars glittering in the sunshine.

The Axis understands thoroughly the crippling result of a successful assault on these plants. Years of unimpeded mass espionage has given them better maps of our industrial dispositions than we possess ourselves. Axis strategists are perfectly aware that our entire system of manufacture is dangerously concentrated in a few cities and that the annihilation of these central targets would see us suddenly paralyzed.

They are certainly planning, scheming and building toward this end, but will hold their hand until a coup of telling proportions can be executed. These men are most unlikely to attempt any minor surprise raid aimed fatuously at our morale alone, with this infinitely more alluring prospect before them.

By far the best method of protection is a web of fighter bases and sound detector systems by which marauders can be intercepted and broken before reaching their objectives.

An important auxiliary method found useful abroad is the dispersal system, by which factory units are broken down into widely separated manufacturing and assembly points. Thus no one ruinous blow can ever remove an entire factory or industry from the national cupboard of assets. All belligerents except ourselves are applying these methods as a principal safeguard. "One famous aircraft manufactory," states Beaverbrook, "is now located in forty-two separate works scattered over four different counties." [12]

The newer strategic plants could be moved far inland and situated in wooded districts or other places of natural concealment. In any case, they should be expertly hidden from all casual view. The European war has developed camouflage and methods for penetrating it, into major arts. The writer has seen concealing netting used in Britain so effectively that what appeared to be a grassy knoll only a hundred yards off, actually masked a substantial factory development. All bases and flying fields are as expertly disguised. It is

[12] April 1941.

almost impossible to distinguish them at a glance from the surrounding farms, and rural estates. Workers' cars as well as army vehicles are invariably painted in divers schemes of concealing coloration so that their presence in numbers does not betray a major point of interest to enemy eyes.

The Germans go in for far more elaborate camouflage. They have disguised an entire lake near Berlin by the use of rafts, so as to draw raiders away from a nearby railway terminal. The Kleine Weser River at Bremen and the Binnen Alster at Hamburg, which are outstanding landmarks in vulnerable areas, were covered with a lattice work "with dummy buildings, trees and a road superimposed to blend in with the surroundings." [13] The Nazis spare no expense and omit nothing that ingenuity can devise to make their camouflage perfect. They even go to the trouble of putting up faked structures to simulate important factories which have been hidden away elsewhere.

Camouflage rarely deceives completely and may be detected by practiced eyes or by various lenses and photographic devices; but it does make identification difficult, thus materially hampering the attackers.

The British have lately taken to building their factories underground. Here they are safe from detection as well as from bombs and bullets of enemy planes. [14] One of these is the world's largest subterranean munitions works. Another sub-surface workshop, an aircraft

[13] Air Commodore H. M. Thornton speaking before the American Society of Newspaper Editors, New York, April 16, 1942.

[14] The cost of building is said to be no greater than of those above ground.

plant, has a total area of several square miles with galleries three-quarters of a mile in length.[15]

The lack of rubber and gasoline for workers' cars might force a shift of industrial expansion toward localities where transportation for labor is good—that is near large metropolitan centers, thus completely defeating the plan for dispersal of industry. This dangerous expedient would set up our vital plants like so many dumb partridges on a limb, ready to be knocked over by the first comer.

If we are to retire behind our own barricades and base our plans entirely on a studied strategy of defense, it would mean that we must abandon the rest of the world to the Axis, who would unquestionably occupy it and incorporate it in its New Order. Our foreign trade would of course disappear entirely with the exception of that with South America, which we should have been compelled to seize outright so as to prevent the possibility of the Axis securing a land base in our hemisphere. We would be forced to find substitutes for all of the critical materials now imported from beyond the geographical limits of the New World.

Our continental mass would become a gigantic fortress under an indefinitely protracted siege, a fantastic double envelopment involving whole continents, which would threaten to close in on us from every direction at once, and which would wait with the patience of a cat at a rat-hole for the moment of internal

[15] Another practice is to build factories and assembly plants into the side of a hill so as to provide a natural bomb-proof shelter.

or strategic weakness when an enormous battering-ram thrust for victory could be successful.

Caught in this grim nutcracker we should be compelled to adopt totalitarian ways, not only as they related to property and labor but also as they concerned free speech and what the Japanese Government has always simply referred to as "dangerous thoughts."

VI. THE BATTLE OF GERMANY

A SECOND and more tolerable view is that we recognize the world as one and indivisible, risking our resources in a great all-out offensive beginning now, in a bold effort to tear out by its roots this cancerous growth which has spread its tentacles over our globe. Only by so doing can we create a life of peace, comfort, decency, and opportunity for ourselves and our children.

Such a course as this requires great risk, unyielding will, and a capacity for intensive organization.

Here, too, everything will depend upon our quick recognition of air power as the single weapon by which domination may be achieved.

Our ability to prevent the consummation of the Axis scheme, unless Russia alone is to win the war for us, is about nil under the types of surface strategy to which we are accustomed.

In every respect but one the Germans have an overwhelming superiority to anything we can offer in the way of organization, instruments of war, effective numbers, position, and communications. The one road open to us for striking at the heart of the Axis war effort, that is, at Germany proper, is through the air. Here alone we could outmatch the Germans in a decisive theater of operations. Here our inventiveness, our industrial capacities, our technological resources, and our *tactical position*, give us the promise of superiority against anything the Germans can do to throw the scales back into balance again. Here alone do the realities of the situation favor us, and then only if we act on them at once.

As far as the military position is concerned, the governing realities are determined by the existence of the British Isles, only a few hundred miles from the German heart of the Axis war effort, *as an advance base for our operations.* The implications of this favorable position have not been generally grasped. Indeed they are being wholly ignored by those who press for "second fronts" in the sense of land invasions.

It is exactly the same as if Germany were able to base herself on Cuba and Long Island at a moment when we were engaged in a savage struggle with some powerful neighbor on our own continent. Imagine that Germany, under those circumstances, were able to devote all her massive resources to the construction of crushing air strength to be hurled at us from these nearby points, to reduce systematically to ashes our railroad yards, docks, communications, factories, warehouses and public utilities—without any fear of effective retaliation. Yet this in sober fact is exactly our position relative to the German Reich.

Combined with the possession of this ideal base the United Nations have at their disposal all the resources necessary for a conclusive operation against the Nazi realm. We can exploit these advantages to win the war in the shortest possible time and at the least cost in life and substance to ourselves—provided we radically alter our conception of the type of task force required, investing all our resources of brains, energy and materials for total assault in the air sphere.

The necessary preparations for such a colossal enterprise are immense. They dwindle to small proportions, however, when contrasted with the enormous apparatus required for sea-borne invasions by millions of soldiers with mountains of equipment, based on vast and complexly organized transport systems.

Everything about the existing situation is providential for our use, a set of circumstances which plays directly into our hands if we possess the imagination and commanding will necessary to utilize them. We have the inventive genius, the skill, the industrial capacity, and the freedom from counter-attack. We have a great, fixed, unsinkable aircraft carrier, right athwart the coast of our main enemy, as a perfect base for short-range operations. We even possess all the available facilities for long-range weather prediction, a factor of increasing consequence in cubic war.[1]

It is a piece of difficult and expensive engineering to construct bombers capable of carrying a payload of explosives across the Atlantic and back. The cost in gasoline, man-hours, engine-energy and raw materials per ton of bombs is staggering compared to that of machines which need only shuttle over a comparatively small neck of territory. One machine attacking Germany from its base in Britain can do the job of twenty forced to make the long haul over the great forbidding waste of sea. Our bombers need only go

---

[1] The exact location of these points constitutes a military secret, but they are located in certain areas in Greenland, Iceland, and the Bering Sea, as well as in other parts of the globe.

240 miles to reach the Ruhr Basin from Dover. Even to strike into the far end of the German industrial complex in the heart of Silesia, they need only travel 650 miles. In order to get at us and reverse this performance, Germany must figure on the following distances: between Brest and Pittsburgh, 3800 miles; between Brest and Gary, Indiana, 4000 miles; between Brest and Birmingham, Alabama, 4300 miles.

Quite different from our own complete freedom of action, the policy of the German Reich is decided for it by geography. Its position on a contiguous land surface alongside of powerful neighbors requires it to keep tremendous military establishments of a fixed type. These draw with omniverous appetite on the lifeblood of the country, absorbing its best minds and the greatest portion of its energies, factory space, manpower and raw materials.

In all of his campaigns the stern pressures of physical reality have forced Hitler to maneuver so as to capture his objectives whole, whereas we need only consider them as targets to be smashed. Except in cases such as Rotterdam, Warsaw, and Belgrade where deliberate terror tactics and berserk Teutonic fury on the loose created a blazing hell of all-out destruction, the *Wehrmacht* has attempted to bag its victims intact so that industries and resources could be taken undamaged. An area taken after being bombarded to bits, its earth scorched black and its cities in ruins, is not an asset but a liability. It has nothing to contribute to the conqueror but the need for policing it.

In this sense both we and the English are in a far more fortunate position, a situation the German

Fuehrer attempted to equalize by his ill-fated adventure in Russia. This was unquestionably the primary reason for Hitler's otherwise inexplicable decision to risk a war on two fronts. As long as the Soviet giant existed he did not dare expend all his energies in the construction of an unfettered air fleet which could attack frontally, take its losses as a matter of course, and duplicate in the cubic sphere the type of roaring, unlimited onslaught for which the Germans are known in surface warfare. By wrecking the potential menace of the Soviet Army the Nazi leader hoped he could free himself from the tyranny of voracious land establishments with their insatiable appetites for oil, men and materials, so as to be able to concentrate his efforts without fear of disastrous consequences, on the creation of that unlimited power he needs to bring the British to their knees.

The inevitability of such a race for air power is well recognized by informed British leaders. Said one of them to the writer: "If we don't blow Germany out of the air the Huns will finally blow England out of the air, and will win the war by literally blowing away our industries and communications until there is nothing left."

We may be certain that the Germans are well aware of the decisive role air power will play and of the precarious position a full-dress air assault would place them in. The unlooked for reversals over Britain as well as the sequence of events following, have made it perfectly clear to the High Command that if it cannot dictate peace terms in the London skies, it cannot dictate them at all.

The Germans know what the issues are and will do their best to meet them; it is fatal to believe otherwise. Everything that has to do with the *Luftwaffe* today benefits from a rigidly enforced priority applying to manpower, appropriations and materials alike. If and when the Nazis beat their Muscovite adversaries down, we may prepare to be shocked by the sudden springing of a gigantic surprise air fleet which will sweep all before it and will allow us no further time for recuperation.

Whatever this dimly lit future may have in store, there is no doubt that at present the British Isles are firmly held under the shield of the Royal Air Force. The Minister for Air, Sir Archibald Sinclair, told the writer last winter that he was certain "the R.A.F. was now superior to the Germans in every department, quantitatively as well as qualitatively." Though that superiority was not sufficiently marked to allow England to take control of the air spaces at points distant from her own bases, raids employing hundreds of British planes, each carrying from two to eight tons of bombs, have become commonplace. Great mass forays involving 1000 or more planes are no longer a startling novelty.

It may be fairly assumed that the drain on Germany's capital for other purposes has been so great that she could hardly have perfected the aviation strength necessary to secure domination of the English skies. And in the meanwhile both British and American production potentials have been developing with impressive speed.

If England should fall, the wholly favorable tactical

position which we now enjoy would at once disappear. We would then face Germany on equal terms except for the relative capacities to produce. Therein lies the urgency of utilizing the current tactical picture without delay. Our strategy against the Axis must be governed by a recognition of the fact that we must take the offensive before the emergence of the great, compact Eurasian-African land mass towards whose staggering manpower and resources the Axis partners are reaching. When this fatal point is reached we can forget all questions of the offensive, since none will be open to us.

The tremendous advantage of being able to throw all we have into Air Power, once we have decided upon that as the most direct course of action, is an obvious one. Germany, irretrievably locked in a gigantic battle on the Eastern front, has little choice and must maintain its array of armed might as long as a single respectable opponent exists adjacent to its borders. Thus it is faced with a sanguinary threat in a decisive theater of action which it cannot possibly answer.

Only in the coming battle of Germany can we settle accounts once and for all with the Axis. The key to the entire edifice of the New Order is the *Reich*. If the Nazi citadel were knocked out, Japan would be left in a hopeless situation. Vast enemy forces would place her long battle lines in a relentless vise. Her grip on Asia would have to be yielded almost at once, and an attack on the main Nipponese islands, similar in scope to that which had previously reduced Germany, would force a speedy decision. Our course against Japan would involve during the whole main period of the coming battle of Germany, no more than a holding action, with airplane and submarine attacks endeavoring to cut the vastly over-extended supply lines which now lead out like a shaky funnel to the south for almost 4000 miles.

We can fight the battle of Germany *now* and win by systematic, grueling destruction over a limited period of time if we turn our energies to the task. At the present time we are producing several hundred four-engine bombers a month, a figure which will soon be raised to 500 a month. Eventually at Willow Run alone, it is predicted by Henry Ford that one of these big machines will be turned out every hour of the day.

A reasonable diversion of our raw materials and industrial energies from other and less critically needed equipment, would enable us to boost the monthly output to several thousand within a year. The rarer metals could be funneled into the bomber program almost in their entirety, without hurt, allowing substitute materials to fill in the void.

Here we have a unique opportunity. If we were to concentrate on the output of heavy bombers on the largest scale of which our industrial economy was capable, for a shattering assault on German communications, industry and morale while the Reich is still inextricably engaged in the East, we could certainly well hope that the effect would be decisive.

To implement this program successfully all civilian and military industries, manufacturing plants and air fields, should be canvassed to see what can be developed speedily in the way of air power if it is given absolute priority on everything, and first access to every resource on the American continent.

A tremendous experimental laboratory would be set up, or a series of these, which would develop newer, larger, and better types, as well as substitute materials. Associated with it would be a proving command which would probe and test every experimental design which offered the promise of merit, testing it out under field conditions, and nursing into maturity those which justified it.

All the bars which now stratify military thinking would be let down. Experimentation would be encouraged in every possible direction, in the belief that American inventive genius and enthusiasm would soon place at our disposal a clear-cut superiority in weapons and means.

We should not wait but should begin now, throwing into the breach everything we have. Our entire available attack force should be based in Britain and flung at the heart and center of the enemy's system, the Reich itself. Whatever we possess in productive strength should be concentrated immediately, with an unswerving singleness of purpose on the job of knocking out Germany by direct and sustained assault from the British Isles. From this point forward the primary aim of the United Nations would be to increase the weight of aerial attack against the Reich at all costs and with the utmost possible speed.

The manufacture of heavy bombers could be centralized in the United States. These would be flown over directly to their operational bases in Britain.

Dovetailing with this effort, the British would concentrate on the building of fighter, pursuit, and interceptor planes, as well as the various types of explosives that would be employed.

The problems of transport would be immeasurably reduced. The only elements in our task force which would have to be convoyed would be ground crews and equipment, replacement parts, and gasoline.

A cardinal difficulty would be the establishment of the elaborate bases required, with their great ground staffs, anti-aircraft batteries, radio-locators, and other necessary paraphernalia. These bases would be the very mainspring of our attack plan and would have to be protected by every device and scheme which ingenuity could invent, including expert camouflage, underground hangars, buried munitions dumps, and hidden supply depots.

The military principles which would govern the technique, strategy and tactics of this proposed campaign are simple. These are:

(1) Wherever two belligerents of comparable power are separated by a body of water which cannot be bridged, the conflict becomes one of air power alone, so that the combatant first able to develop an overwhelming assault by the use of air strength will, with absolute certainty, finally succeed in grinding his opponent to bits.

(2) A national organism is like any other living body. If the heart or vitals are pierced, the limbs or periphery immediately proceed to die or dry up. No matter how much territory or resources Nazi Germany held fast in her grip, even were she able to conquer

all Europe, Asia and Africa, if desperate and deadly blows were struck at her vitals—at her transportation centers, factory concentrations, and civilian morale—it would mean the quick and complete disintegration of her entire war effort.

(3) All forces which can possibly be brought to bear should be at the point where the decisive blows are to be struck, even at the risk of weakness at other points. An air offensive, to be successful, cannot be a mere harassing affair. It must be an attack in force comparable to any other type of all-out campaign. It should accept the necessity of heavy losses just as this is accepted in a great land operation.

The British boasted while the writer was in London that they had dropped some 10,000 tons of high explosives on the enemy within a period of three months. Compared to the amount of munitions—and lives— which would have been used up in a massive land attack, this must be regarded as a minor operation. Yet the damage inflicted has been increasingly effective. The British air force, in fact, is the only weapon which has brought the war home to the Germans and served to relieve them of any over-confidence they might possess in its outcome.

It is difficult to tell in specific detail what the results of these raids have been. The Nazis are always at great pains to clean up the debris quickly. The shattered places are made tidy and if possible turned into parks—largely for the psychological value involved.

The best sources of information are the checks made by British photographer-pilots. The writer has seen pictures showing whole sections of such cities as Aachen and Hamm literally razed to the ground. Almost one-half of Aachen and Münster have been demolished. Cologne, capital of the Ruhr, was hit by over 140 raids before the gigantic foray of May 31, 1942. Whole acres of the city lie in waste, with the power station and leading manufactories wrecked. The important railway junction of Mannheim has an area of some 30,000 square yards in the very center of the city flattened out like a pancake. Its railway yards have been badly jumbled more than once due to direct hits, and various assembly points and armored-car and machine-tool factories reduced to twisted brick and steel. On one occasion the city was left burning from one end to the other, its water mains destroyed. As a result of rail damage it is reported that the time required for a car to pass through the yard had increased by the end of December from eight hours to seven days. As an indirect result the yards at Basle, 160 miles away, became blocked. Whole trains of freight cars in the Moselle and Saar region, loaded with bauxite and iron ore, have been held up for over a month in trying to approach Mannheim.

Berlin itself has been given substantial attention and its whole ring of workshops, arsenals, mills and factories—producers of motors, heavy guns, engines, tanks and hydraulic presses—was impartially potted. The enormous Klingenberg power station supplying much of the city's industrial light and power, was given a rough going-over. For a considerable period the Berlin subway was put out of commission.

The great northern ports of Wilhelmshaven, Kiel,

Bremen and Hamburg, where the submarines are made, have been raided hundreds of times and present a pathetic picture with whole sections gutted. There is hardly a place in Hamburg which does not have its area of devastation. A single demolition charge destroyed 25,000 square yards in the heart of the town's industrial district, and damaged every structure within 80,000 square yards. In January 1942, alone, the Bomber Command was over Hamburg on ten nights, setting enormous conflagrations, damaging docks, and flattening whole blocks of houses. The shipyards at Kiel were so badly blasted that "the only way to put out the fires would have been to push the whole place into the sea." [2] Power stations were destroyed and entire residential sections had to be evacuated.

The port of Lübeck received such a lacing on a single night that forty per cent of the old inner town was laid in ruins. Row after row of buildings were left with only the walls standing, and the streets were impassable with twisted debris. Warehouses, factories and port facilities were all heavily struck. The same unhappy fate befell another large Baltic port, Rostock. The big Focke-Wulf factory at Bremen was annihilated, as well as other aircraft plants, submarine works and war equipment manufactories. A Scandinavian traveler said of the city that "the center of Bremen simply doesn't exist any more." [3]

[2] Report of a returning pilot.

[3] A comparable raid, late in April 1942, on the German submarine base at Trondheim which had taken 5000 Danish workers two years to build, was undertaken by seventy-five heavy British bombers which utterly destroyed it in less than two hours.

The raid on Paris by British planes on March 3, 1942, also lasted

As early as 1940 the R.A.F. was smashing away at the Ruhr district with its sprawled out iron, steel and coal industries, and its great arsenals and chemical factories. Despite all precautions and defenses, bombing planes get through, cracking down on factories and communication points. Prior to the massive attack of June 1, 1942, a single raid blew up the main power station at Essen, with 2200 casualties. The families of workers throughout the length and breadth of this area have been evacuated. The big Krupp works at Essen has been struck innumerable times and utterly devastated. The great Thyssen Steel Works near Hamborn, with a production of over a million tons a year, is being systematically and progressively demolished. This strategic area, about two-thirds the size of Long Island, once held the largest part of Germany's coal, pig iron, steel, and tin plate, as well as a big slice of her heavy manufactories. Even steel plates for submarines are made here and sent all the way to the shipbuilding yards at Kiel and Hamburg.

No one knows precisely how much dislocation to their war effort this long-continued pounding has cost the Germans. It must have seriously disturbed their ability to bring goods to the all-important eastern front. Its effect on morale must have been marked. It has caused a great, painful trek eastward of vital war industries seeking to escape the effective range of the relentless night raider. It has immobilized a good part

two hours and was made by a force which spokesmen said was not exceptionally large. Six hundred people were killed; over 1000 wounded. Returning pilots and bombardiers said that at the great Renault plant and other heavy-duty manufactories, bombs scattered buildings "like packs of cards."

of the *Luftwaffe*—Lord Halifax asserted that these incursions "forced Germany to keep in the West half its available fighters when they would otherwise have been flung into the great battles on the Russian front."

Even though the damage inflicted by present limited methods seems to have been considerable, such raids are at best experimental forays, precursors of the fabulously destructive processions which are to follow.

Our campaign must rest on a planned operation seeking complete and conclusive victory. It must not be conceived as a preliminary action but as a knockout blow, justifying a large investment of equipment and a far-reaching diversion to aviation of production now directed to other channels. The policy must be to hit the Germans in Germany. The task is the single one of concentrating all available air power and the increasing flow of new production on the main German target. We should seek to avoid a war of attrition or a painfully slow period of extensive blood-letting. The campaign should be designed for a quick death blow, for victory within a period of months—at the most a year.

Bombing, without plan and without continuity, cannot produce the results desired. Only a continuous scheme of destruction based on a systematic reduction of communication centers, viaducts and bridges, shipyards, key factories, oil reservoirs, and industrial aggregates, can defeat the enemy by making it impossible for him to carry on.

Our ultimate goal as the grand finale of the great operation should be a continuously replenished pool of 5000 heavy bombers weighing up to 300 tons each, with speeds in excess of 400 miles per hour.[4] Whether or not we reach this goal is not as important as that we drive rigorously toward it. Five thousand Consolidated B-24's or Boeing B-17E's would serve our purpose nicely and would do a first-class job in reducing Germany to a pulp. Invention and technical progress will inevitably bring us to the heavier faster ship but we need not wait for that—as long as we possess numbers and a willingness to use them.

A sky battlefleet of the proportions proposed, coupled with a readiness to write off 2500 of the craft a month, would for the first time constitute an aerial body capable of delivering an attack in force, so as to be able to compel an absolute decision with no other important supplementary factors operating.

As long as the Russian front remained active, this growing armada would function in effect as the co-operative unit in a gigantic land-air action. A true and practical "second front" would thus be opened up. Here would be a piece of co-ordination between ground and air forces conceived on a grand strategic scale, and worthy of the first-class military mind! Thus those who have been crying for a complementary or auxiliary front in the West would find their vision indulged by a great master operation on a magnificent

[4] Glenn Martin has already announced that he is prepared to build a plane weighing 250 tons and carrying a payload of eighty tons, whenever such a ship becomes desirable from the military view.

The Douglas B-19, a purely experimental model, is capable of a flight to Europe and return with some 30,000 pounds of bombs.

Another large American company is understood to have a prototype craft under construction which would carry fifty tons of high explosives across the ocean with ease.

scale, the whole action perfectly synchronized with the strategy of the Russian ground troops. Since there is no practical necessity for such a second action-phase to be in some special sphere such as ground or water, there appears to be no reason why it may not be opened in the only zone in which we possess the superiority of striking power—the air.

Air power alone, completely unassisted by other arms, could certainly gain the decision. But if a co-operative action, in which all arms are engaged, is necessary to secure agreement, there can be no reason against it, since the Russian armies are already on the battle lines with the major portion of their equipment and will not have to be transported. Such a co-operation phase need cause very little dislocation in the basic plan of vertical envelopment and would have the virtue of eliminating the familiar argument used against airplanes—that they have no occupying power and hence are incapable of gaining a decision. The conventional view remains that in order to achieve final victory it is necessary to defeat the enemy army in the field, though a study of the last war gives no support to this contention. It was lost by a nation whose armed forces had not been conclusively beaten and who was standing on foreign territory on every front at the moment of capitulation; and, remarks Douhet, it was almost won by the defeated nation through the use of submarines possessing no occupying power whatsoever.[5]

---

[5] Professor Banse wept that had the German Admiralty taken full advantage of their opportunities, building U-boat after U-boat instead of slavishly attempting to ape the British in the question of

The argument that completely self-contained air campaigns cannot obtain a decision because Hitler failed to do so in the Battle of Britain is silly. History is full of examples of strategies which failed, often as not for an insufficient concentration of force at the critical point. This was the case at the Battle of the Marne in the World War, where the German High Command dispersed its forces over two fronts, ignoring the death-bed warning of Count Schlieffen, whose last words were: "*Keep your right wing strong.*" Pure accident decided the case at Waterloo, where Marshal Ney's instructions to D'Erlon inadvertently canceled Bonaparte's orders and deprived the French attack of the necessary punch to turn an orderly retreat into a rout. Napoleon's failure to defeat the Allied forces in detail while he had the opportunity, may be compared to the success of the Romans in beating Hasdrubal at Metaurus, preventing a fatal junction of the two Carthaginian brothers who would then have had Italy at their mercy.

For absolute and conclusive effect air power must be something more than mere desultory pinpricking. Factories, cities, and communication centers may be pretty badly smashed and the damage still be repairable. The rehabilitating quality of cities and industrial establishments is in this sense comparable to the recuperative power of man himself. But there is a point where cities, industrial installations, water works, and strategic arteries may no longer be profitably repaired. It is at this point that they must be abandoned, and

battleships, unrestricted submarine warfare would have determined the conflict.—*Germany Prepares for War*, p. 137.

if the aerial arm is to achieve victory it should have at its disposal sufficiently heavy forces to exploit to the absolute limit any success it is able to create.

It was conceded in Britain by military men whose authority the writer must respect, that had the Germans been able to carry on in an increasing crescendo of fury during the Battle of Britain for another ten days, England might have been forced to capitulate. The fact of the matter was that the Nazis were simply unable to accept their losses and continue. Even an unconditional surrender by Britain, had the issue been forced, would have left Hitler with a skeleton air arm and hence helpless against Russia in the East if the Muscovite giant had chosen that moment in which to leap. The Germans could not afford a victory in the British Isles at the risk of losing air command over the Continent.

A concentration on other people's failures does not lead to any useful result. The fact that gallant Chungking was able to take its beating from the Japanese air force without wincing, proves nothing. In a great country like China, not well organized industrially and economically, no nerve ganglia exist which can be speedily put out of operation. No reasonable comparison may be made between it and such states as Germany or France, either of which could succumb to a blitz attack within a matter of weeks. In a highly organized country where all services, industries, and communications radiate to central points, the entire pattern of existence would be hopelessly disrupted if these control centers were systematically flattened out. The psychological result would be equal to the physical. The sense of frustration, of being hammered without being able to hammer back, is an element of destructive power in itself which works for the attackers.

The failure of aerial assault to break the will of the enemy despite intensive bombing and the employment of systematic terrorism, is attributable to two reasons:

(1) If it is applied to a country of peasants instead of to a highly industrialized nation whose nerve centers lie completely exposed to attack, no great control switch exists by which chaos and collapse can be induced. Resistance then continues on a decentralized or guerrilla basis, as in Serbia or China, a situation whose difficulty increases with the size of the area in which it is operative.

(2) The results of limited bombing in a complexly organized state have been to harden the population and to make its will-to-continue even greater than before. In this case the morale factor is one of contact and ideas, disintegrating finally with the collapse of the controlling social and economic structure.

In its basic properties the air sphere is no different from any other. No case of absolute certainty can be made out for it under all conditions. War here is like war in any other dimension—it is the law of probabilities or the capacity for making use of slight or transient advantages which indicates the genius of the commander. And wherever heavy gains are sought, heavy risks are unavoidable.

British airmen are altogether convinced of the possibility this situation offers. The Minister of Airplane Production and Supply, Moore Brabizon, confidently told the author: "Our tanks will walk across Europe if we can clear the air." And Air Marshal Sir Sholto Douglas [6] commented: "The war will be won by the time we are able to invade the Continent."

Like the opinions of airmen everywhere, their views are baldly expressed, and to the point. The writer mentioned to a friend in the Air Ministry that serious tracts were still being written in America covering cavalry maneuver and prodded him for comment. His reply condensed a volume of opinion in a single sentence. Said he dryly: "Yes, yes, I know, old fellow! The order will be 'The horse will now attack assisted by two squadrons of Spitfires and one of Hurricanes!' "

II

Germany for the first time finds herself engaged in a war of nerves with virtually the whole initiative of action on a decisive front in the hands of an opponent. The enormous area on which the *Wehrmacht* sits must be defended; the extensive demands of the eastern theater makes the presence of air units mandatory, forcing a fatal dispersal of the Reich's air fleets. The advantage of feinting thrusts directed from Britain are all in the hands of the United Nations whose factual striking power is hence out of all proportion to its arithmetical superiority of planes and position.

The United Nations have come a long way since Goering's pompous boast that he had investigated the situation thoroughly and guaranteed in person that no

[6] Chief of the Fighter Command.

hostile airplane could ever get through to the Ruhr. "Berliners had been assured that no enemy plane could penetrate the multiple rings of anti-aircraft defenses which stood between Berlin and the Western frontiers." [7] The Germans were totally unprepared for such an onslaught. "It came as a shuddering mental shock. Their invincibility had been penetrated. It was a straw in the wind, but a straw which pointed inexorably to the way whereby Germany can be conquered." [8] For the first time in 130 years Germans, who had been carrying the horrors of war to the territories of other peoples, feel the weight of them now on their own heads. Doubt exists throughout the Reich. There have been cases of hysterical development among the population, which had to be put down by the police. When the writer left Europe last winter, Goebbels was already calling on the frightened *herrenvolk* to be calm, attempting to shame them by pointing out the British as an example of fortitude under fire.

As the weight of attack increases the blueprint of strategic operation alters. Previously it had been concerned with retaliation, the smashing of key factories, submarine bases and other targets, and the embroilment of a large number of German planes which had at any cost to be kept from the Russian front.

With the entire fury of aerial assault unleashed, the scheme changes from one of secondary activity to a primary action designed to dissolve resistance directly and force a conclusion.

[7] Harsch, *Pattern of Conquest*, pp. 28, 29, 30.
[8] Ibid., p. 33.

There are several methods by which this can be achieved. One is an attempted destruction of the industrial base of the enemy, demolishing his war materials at their source. This involves a complex activity moving in a great many levels and directions. Factories manufacturing key equipment such as the Siemens Electrical Works in Berlin, and the Zeiss Instrument Works at Jena, can be sought out. The elimination of minor instruments can break the whole chain of action in a great industry, forcing the other component portions of the structure into idleness. Assembly points can be put out of existence, as was the immense Heinkel plant at Rostock. Such vital areas as the Ruhr can be gone at systematically, with the knowledge that this tremendous area of belching black smoke and great processing plants can neither be abandoned nor moved without prohibitive cost.[9]

Like the English, the Germans are attempting to meet this onslaught in part by building their factories and assembly points under ground, in the sides of hills, or hidden in forests. They are making a feverish effort to decentralize their industries so as to lessen their attractiveness as targets, and have been actively at work moving them to the east, out of closely knit zones. One of the new districts is on the lower Elbe River, another back of the Sudeten Mountains. Since even this zone of safety has been found vulnerable, the newest movement is far to the east, a dispersion belt

[9] The Ruhr is an almost solidly built-up area, running eastward from Duisburg to Dortmund—a continuous mass of towns, factories, and industrial plants. Here are many of the heavy industries utterly necessary to the German war effort.

which reaches from upper Silesia to Krakow, and thence to the southeast of what was formerly Poland.

An important series of objectives are the electrical power plants already under heavy pressure to expand their generating capacities under the voracious demands of wartime industries. A secondary string of targets would be gas works, storage places, oil reservoirs and water supply systems.

To make this campaign effective it must be controlled by a careful reconnaissance and espionage system which seeks out the weak links in the German economy, which knows just what stocks of critical materials are in existence and their relationship in terms of space, time and production to the Nazi war effort.

A project which offers more attractive prospects for quick and conclusive results is the vertical blockade directed at the communication and transport systems which have been the heart of all German operations on the Continent since the days of von Moltke. The Nazi military oracle, Professor Banse, called warfare "largely a matter of transport facilities." [10] Hitler, alleging that the Russians were already beaten, asserted that "the bringing up of our supplies to date is just a matter of transportation." [11]

· An all-out assault on the highly developed network of German roads, railways and canals, freightyards, bridges and viaducts, would, if persisted in, pile up traffic and communications generally so as actually to

[10] *Germany Prepares for War*, p. 48.
[11] October 4, 1941.

bring about the failure of the entire German war economy.

The farther the Germans go from their industrial centers, the greater the strain on their transportation and manufacturing facilities. The destruction of irreplaceable rolling stock is an element of serious worry to the German high command. The railway system breaks down continually due to being overloaded. The jumble which extends to all points of destination as the result of a freight tie-up, vastly widens the area of wasted time. Schedules can no longer be adhered to. The dislocation spreads out fanwise to the fighting fronts, to the factories and to all other zones of consumption. The result of even the limited offensive so far undertaken has been to create an acute shortage of freight cars. Long distance transport of certain commodities has actually been forbidden. Part of the German failure in Russia represents a crisis in the transportation problem—a maze of congestion which the circuitous rerouting caused by British bombing continually adds to.

The German railway system is a criss-crossing plexus which is a direct result of the Teuton passion for order and regimentation. In the Ruhr there are more than twenty-five miles of railroad to each hundred square miles. Every important city in the country is the hub of a great railroad wheel and can be reached from any one of a half a dozen directions. In addition, there are a great many lesser towns which are the juncture of two or more railroads.[12]

[12] The major railway centers of west Germany are Münster, Hamm, Duisburg, Düsseldorf, Cologne, Frankfort-am-Main, Mann-

These railway centers lie in a radius of 200 to 600 miles from Dover, with the more critically important cities all less than 400 miles away.

Germany also relies heavily on her canal system, especially for the handling of such cargo as coal, ore, oil, and lumber. Maximum use is made of the inland waterways in order to reduce the strain on the overtasked railroads as much as possible. A shining objective is the Dortmund-Ems Canal which connects the industrial Ruhr with northwestern Germany, running into the sea at Emden. It carries the equivalent of several hundred trainloads daily. Its docks and lockgates make splendid targets; and if the two aqueducts which carry the canal across the River Ems could be destroyed, this artery would be cut entirely.

Another artery which should draw the unwelcome attention of the big bombers is the Danube. Even more important is the extensive Russian network which connects Odessa on the Black Sea with Danzig in the North through the rivers Pripet, Bug, Vistula and Dnieper. These waterways are one of the main German communications and should be a primary object of attack.

By bombing the canal system and oil barges which bring Rumanian oil to the reservoirs and dispersal points, and by simultaneously dissolving railway junctions and yards which control traffic to the Balkans, an ominous oil shortage would be brought about.

heim, and Karlsruhe. In south Germany they are Augsburg, München, Regensburg, Stuttgart, and Nuremberg. In central Germany they are Mainz, Erfurt, Hanover, Halle, Kassel, Leipzig, Dresden, Berlin. In north Germany they are Hamburg and Stettin, and in east Germany Frankfurt-am-Oder and Breslau.

The oil would not necessarily have to be destroyed. Merely the inability of the *Wehrmacht* to receive it would be sufficient to produce an identical result. The same is true in relation to all other commodities, whether raw stuffs or completed instruments of war.

The Nazis are consuming oil in the Russian campaign at the rate of 1,500,000 tons a month. Domestic needs boost this total to 2,000,000 tons. The situation is given in a report by the Bureau of Mines which declares that the German petroleum problem appears to be largely one of rationing and administration, and that "Germany seems to be in no immediate danger of the failure of her military machine for lack of gasoline and lubricants." But if the exports from the Rumanian fields, which must make a trip of some 950 miles along the canals can be halted by sustained attack, and if the supplementary rail system can be made the victim of a simultaneous vertical ambush, the Germans would face an immediate stringency in oil. It would be more difficult to seek out and bomb the individual plants which produce petroleum from lignite or extract it from hydro-carbons.[13] These, however, are close to existing industrial centers and can be rendered helpless by annihilating the giant power plants in the lignite area of central Germany.

If Hamm, the great railway junction which controls traffic routed through western Germany to the eastern front, could be destroyed it would constitute, in itself, a victory of some size. If the yards and warehouses of Mannheim, the junction which regulates

[13] The Reich's total output of synthetic oil is in the neighborhood of 3,500,000 tons annually.

traffic to Italy, were blasted at the same time, the triumph would be of major importance. A really heavy assault on the Ruhr, only 240 miles from Dover, would have a far-reaching effect on the outcome of the war. Berlin itself, only 520 miles from Dover, is an easily accessible target to the determined night raider. It is the hub of many railroads and electric power stations, as well as a vital production center for heavy guns, radio equipment, aircraft and motors. If the same havoc could be played here that the Germans did to Rotterdam, it would be the most significant victory of the war.[14]

The long autumn nights will bring every city in the Reich under the range of the night bombers, enabling them to pay their visits and return before dawn. Aachen and Düsseldorf are only 225 miles from Dover. Bremen is 300 miles from Yarmouth. The heavily industrialized region of Saxony is no more than 500 miles from Dover. Even former Polish-administered Danzig is but 700 miles from Yarmouth.

III

It is certain that the striking power of aircraft is just at the beginning of its development, and that before this war is over there will be startling new forms of design and radically altered tactics, infinitely more efficient and deadly than any now known. The technique of land operations is based on instruments which

[14] At the bombing of Rotterdam, conducted as an object lesson in intimidation, the city was gutted and 30,000 helpless Dutchmen were killed in less than twenty minutes.

have arrived somewhere near their development peak. The tank cannot go over 100 tons, the battleship over 75,000 tons. "On the other hand airplanes in quantity, size, speed, radius of action and ceiling may yet soar to almost fantastic comparative proportions." [15]

New and revolutionary designs are under consideration in all countries, always with a view to superior armament, maneuverability, weight and flexibility of firepower, in an effort to eliminate all blind spots. Eight-engine bombers are being projected, as well as six-engine types with various combinations of pusher and tractor propellers. Italy is experimenting with a new propellerless secret plane for which Italian engineers claim possibilities which verge on the fantastic.[16]

A new type of airplane, superior in speed, maneuverability and firepower, would establish absolute control of the air within a few weeks, provided no use had been made of it until a great surprise squadron could be thrown at the enemy. Methods for extracting such light metals as magnesium and beryllium, or any improved process of manufacture, would give an immeasurable advantage to the side possessing them, if they were promptly exploited. If, for example, beryllium could be alloyed with pure aluminum, it would produce an alloy of revolutionary lightness and strength. Such an alloy would reduce the present

[15] Lieut. Col. Harold E. Hartney, *Flying* Magazine, November 1941.

[16] The ship sucks in air through an opening in its nose, where the air is compressed, passed through a tunnel in the fuselage, and is then expelled in a powerful jet through the tail. High speeds were not attempted in the experimental model.

wing-loading by at least half and by reducing weight, help to increase speed up to 600 miles per hour in level flight.[17]

General Douhet's prediction of a combined bombing and combat plane, a so-called battleplane, could easily become an established fact, upsetting the entire war. Losses in day bombers are due to the low speed now imposed on these craft. If a bomber could be made which would actually fly faster than the interceptor, it would have the air to itself. The creation of a super dreadnought[18] of the sky would enable the invading air fleet to systematically engage the enemy in daylight operations, seeking it out and destroying it as well as its airdromes and bases. The control of Germany itself would then become a mathematical certainty. Such a ship would be able to handle much heavier firepower than could be brought up against it by the small fighter, and could afford to carry the necessary gunners and ammunition as well.

Arnold and Eaker suggest that in the very near future substratosphere flying will move into stratosphere flying.[19] Ranges of 50,000 feet are now made entirely possible by super-chargers and pressure cabins. The battle area of the future could easily climb to 60,000 feet, some ten miles or more above the earth.[20] Once this problem were completely solved it would be easy

[17] Major Charles Malone, *Flying* Magazine, December 1941.

[18] Vincent Burnelli has designed a fighter-bomber combination for which a top speed of 450 miles per hour is anticipated. Other manufacturers have plans already on paper, looking toward a top speed as high as 500 miles per hour.

[19] *Winged Warfare.*

[20] Kettering and his associates are experimenting with pressure cabins to enable a ceiling of 55,000 feet.

for large bombers to ascend completely out of the range of attack, whether by air or from the ground.

Major de Seversky sees a great battleship of the air, developing 32,000 horsepower with a circumglobular range and carrying 100 tons of high explosives. "Long-range air power," he believes, "has been retarded by lack of military imagination rather than aerodynamic obstacles."

Until recently the average, first-class fighter plane was not able to remain in the air more than a few hours at full throttle, and hence was unable to accompany bombers on long-range operations. This fault is being rapidly remedied. The new Westland Whirl-wind, a single-seater, two-engine fighter, is said to have accompanied raiders as far as Cologne, and carries four 20-millimeter cannon bunched in the nose of the fuselage. This development is matched by the U. S. Lockheed P-38, with a range of more than 1000 miles, a speed of over 410 miles per hour, and a ceiling of 40,000 feet.

These developmental possibilities are no mere conjectures for the distant future. They are even now being worked out on the drafting boards. They are in prospect, not only in our own secret laboratories but in those of the enemy.[21] The *Luftwaffe* is already

[21] As time goes on the great loss the German nation suffered in all branches of learning by its expulsion of free scientific minds will begin to be felt. The Nazis have applied and are utilizing for their own purposes the genius of an earlier era of free scientific thinking. As a famous Swiss economist remarked to the author: "They are now living off their fat."

The quality of German laboratory and scientific work has strongly deteriorated and research has lost its brilliance and initiative. In particular, the science of physics has suffered. All this lack will have its effect on the armament of tomorrow.

claimed to be using a new rocket launching device which can toss fighter planes to a height of several thousand feet at 400 miles per hour. The use of rockets in assisted take-off enables the twin-engine Junkers 88-A6 to lift an additional load of more than 3000 pounds. The British also are now utilizing rocket-aided take-offs.

In the field of firepower, expansion is especially rapid. The Russians now carry anti-tank cannon with armor-piercing shells, in their planes. The Brewster Buffalo and Grumman Wildcat mount four .50 caliber guns, which are claimed to have twice the firepower of the eight batteries of British Spitfire and Hurricane types. The new Curtiss P-47 will be still more powerful and is reputed to be by far the most dangerous competitor in the whole arena of fighting ships.

One zone of development where we have an immeasurable advantage lies in the manufacture of 100 and higher octane fuel. The best our enemies possess is 90 octane gas, which allows us an additional performance of well over twenty-five per cent. When we can manufacture fuels of still higher octane rating in service quantities, that advantage will swell to enormous proportions.[22]

[22] What this means in terms of actual performance is quoted by R. McCormick in *Collier's*, February 21, 1942. A 1750 horsepower motor designed for 92 octane gas will weigh around 3500 pounds. A 1750 horsepower motor designed for 100 octane gas will weigh about 2800 pounds.

McCormick quotes the report of Dr. Gustav Egloff who directed fuel experiments on a Dutch Koolhoren FK-59. Using 87 octane gas, the rate of climb at 6500 feet was 1.630, and the time of climb was 4.2 minutes. This compares with the results using 100 octane gas

The huge aerial task force toward whose final creation our productive capacities would be turned, would strike with much the same tactics as a naval squadron, modified by the addition of a third dimension and greatly increased mobility.

The weight of the attack will be computed by reference to a set of actuarial tables created for this purpose. It has long been observed that results increase at a much greater rate than the arithmetic rate of bombing effort. Doubling the number of attackers causes more than twice the damage previously produced, though the exact relation is as yet obscure. Similarly, the greater the weight of the attack, the smaller the proportionate loss to the attacker. The enemy's fire brigades, pursuits and gun crews are pushed beyond their efficiency points and begin to suffer the evils of distraction and overwork. If the increase in bomber numbers and load were to approximate a slope of thirty degrees, the increased angle of effectiveness would rapidly approach forty-five degrees. After a certain point in fatigue is reached the defending fleet starts to deteriorate rapidly. The beginning of the end is then in sight.

Preceding the main fleet would be an advance guard of guerrilla bombers. Some will come moving in on a low level track, like unholy wraiths which are seen and gone in the same instant. Others will come hurtling in at great altitudes. These would be small and fast and capable of moving with such speed that de-

with a rate of climb of 2.360 and a time of climb of 2.9 minutes. The service ceiling, using the 110 octane gas, rose from 31,800 feet to 35,700, and the absolute ceiling from 32,800 to 36,700.

fending fighters with the most rapid rate of climb, would find the damage done and the quarry gone before they could get at him. Such craft would be built of plywood, or some light, tough alloy, with the rear turrets and armor sacrificed for speed. Only the bulkhead and a 30-degree cone covering the front and rear axis aft would carry protective plate. These craft would be regarded as expendable ammunition if necessary, and would spread out in widely separated areas in a gigantic feinting operation, scattering incendiaries broadcast and lighting great fires to serve as a guide for the big bombers which followed. Everything which could burn would be subject to military arson, including the extensive German forests, forcing a condition of indescribable confusion and anxiety on the beleaguered enemy.

At the core of each formation would be the fast, heavy, possibly unarmed bomb carriers delivering lethal loads of fifty tons or more. In strange contrast with the familiar multi-gunned juggernauts full of gadgets and with big crews to work them, this type would be simply a shell built around the biggest projectiles attainable and made as fast as possible, without an ounce of instrumentation not directly required by its mission.

These craft would be flanked by flying machine guns and artillery platforms equipped with three- and six-inch guns—long-range fighters and interceptors of great combat strength and maneuverability. These twin-engine pursuits would carry a pilot and two gunners. Twelve synchronized machine guns of heavy caliber would blaze away out of the leading edge, with two more in a blister just back of the pilot. Several free-firing cannon would be located in the nose. The rear would be protected by a nest of flexible machine guns. Its rate of climb would be prodigious and it would be able to power-dive at more than 700 miles per hour. Its forward speed at full throttle would be around 500 miles per hour.

Lighter and medium size bombers capable of carrying five to twenty tons each of effective load, bristling with machine guns and carrying three 75-millimeter cannon firing fore and aft, would fly in convoying echelons. They would be armored throughout with face-hardened plate,[23] and after dropping their charges of explosive would become fast and formidable fighters, easily a match for any interceptors which might come up against them.

In a large co-ordinated action there would be two types of fighters used—one a general purpose and the other a high altitude fighter, both possessing range far beyond that now existing. The plane of the future will want the greatest possible simplicity of controls and instrument arrangement. The instruments would have all needles normally at one level, so that if anyone on the panel were out of line it would be instantly apparent that something was wrong. This would enable the pilot, especially in the small pursuit, to keep his mind on his opposite number up there in the air without dangerous distraction.[24]

[23] This plate has an extremely hard outer-surface for about 25 per cent of its thickness, with a much softer and ductile under-surface. When hit by an armor-piercing ball the usual dangerous splintering of the steel does not take place.

[24] Several possible arrangements have been suggested, such as providing a horn or red light to indicate a danger zone.

The invading fleet would be broken into various-sized elements, each with its appointed task and under the command of its own officer, who would give his orders by interplane radio-telephone. These planes, the flagships of the fleet, would carry radio locators to indicate the approach of hostile craft. The swarm would come in silently at great altitude, in formations designed to offer maximum protection to the principal bomb carriers at its center. When the target is reached the squadrons would break formation and the tactics of assault would begin. While the principal bombers made for the major objective, the medium and lighter craft would scatter for an assault on secondary targets.

A typical raiding group could be made up as follows: About 600 fighter and interceptor planes with a range equal to the task before them, heavily armored on all vital surfaces and possessing the superiority in firepower essential for temporary control of the air over the site of operations. Fast single-seaters working in co-ordination with big multiple-engine fighters carrying heavy cannon, would dart in and out of position in a tactical scheme calculated to cover the operations of the super-bombers at the center and to protect all "blind spots" by maneuver.

In our hypothetical formations there would be twenty such great flying bombloads. Each would carry fifty tons or more of high explosives. Along with them would be 150 medium bombers bearing twenty tons apiece, and 300 light bombers carrying five tons per machine. This would provide an approximate load

of 5500 tons of annihilating fury for a single raid.[25]
Such a devastating barrage of demolition would cut
any possible series of targets into ribbons, leaving nothing standing and nothing alive in its path.

The effect of such assaults may be compared with
the German raids on London, where in the heaviest
of all single attacks [26] less than 500 tons of explosives
were dropped all told, no single one larger than 2000
pounds. On only one other occasion did the *Luftwaffe*
drop as much as 400 tons in a single night. The long-
remembered incursion on Coventry, which reduced
that important little city to a mass of ruins in two
nights, involved no more than 300 tons of bombs.

Those who underestimate the effectiveness of bombing on the basis of the British experience should remember that we have only seen the earliest part of
the development cycle of this new terror. R.A.F. bomb
carriers which early in 1941 furtively darted out of the
night, few in number and carrying but a few thousand
tons of bombs, none of which weighed over 500
pounds, now sweep in in great formations numbering
from 300 to 1000. Craft like the Sterling can carry a
demolition charge up to eight tons, with individual
bombs weighing up to 4000 pounds each. The shatter
power of one of these is sufficient to make an overhead cover of more than 100 feet necessary in all
shelters.

Various new types of explosives continue to make

[25] The assault on Cologne of May 31, 1942, involved 1130 planes
and the use of 3000 tons of high explosives. That on Essen two days
later almost equaled these figures.

[26] May 10, 1941.

their appearance and are being experimented with. TNB, a sister compound to TNT, develops a pressure twenty-five per cent greater under identical conditions.[27] Nitrogen bombs have shown furious destructive force, though only used in comparatively small capsules. Liquid oxygen has been described as presenting many advantages over TNT, as have such new compounds as pentaerythritetetranitrate.

According to the most up-to-date curves, the peak of destruction-efficiency is reached with a single ten-ton projectile, after which the curve falls off. It is entirely conceivable that the shatter power of such a monster could be wickedly increased by the addition of rocket propulsion,[28] or the perfection of any one of a number of processes now being studied in laboratories all over the world.

It is difficult to tell what the effect of such vicious missiles would be, but it may be assumed that in conjunction with a thorough broadcast of incendiaries, they will reduce any city or industrial settlement to the dimensions of rubble. Theoretically a demolition charge of such proportions would knock out the entire center of Berlin. It is conceivable that such a ten-ton load would topple buildings within a radius of miles and people would lie dead, huddled in their cellars, their lungs and eardrums burst by concussion, much as fish are killed in ponds by the illegal dynamite sticks of poachers.

An insight into the future effect of monster bomb

[27] Tenney L. Davis, *Chemistry of Powder and Explosives.*
[28] The increase of speed added to its mass raises the destructive fury of the charge upwards in geometric ratio.

loads is gained from an article which appeared in the London *Lancet* on October 11, 1941, detailing the effects of a land mine which had dropped close to a wooden hut housing some soldiers. The explosion was of such violence as to shake a hospital over two miles away. The hut itself was completely demolished. A considerable proportion of the men were found dead with little evidence of external injury. Autopsies, however, showed ruptured eardrums, hemorrhages into the substance of the lung tissue, and evidence of extreme shock. Those who did not immediately die developed symptoms similar to pneumonia—prostration, shock, and extreme respiratory difficulty.

The scheme of action and the tactical possibilities which present themselves have been given here merely in outline. There are many variations and refinements of technique which would be worked out by the applying military mind, which would endeavor to reduce the theoretical postulates of cubic war to a controlled science. There is no reason, for instance, why there should not be a transference to purely aerial operations of combat team tactics. The prospect is by no means bizarre. Just as dive-bombers precede the main attack to put opposing artillery out of commission, special types of bombing and assault planes could precede the storming armada of the air in order to silence the ground artillery and ack-ack guns. It must be taken for granted that there is no type of ordnance which cannot be immobilized for at least a short space through a concentration of forces and a readiness to accept initial losses as a justifiable investment.

already a shell-shocked people. They have passed through enormous revolutionary changes in which great elements of the population have been suppressed and their activities strangulated—the Lutherans, Catholics, Socialists, Democrats, Free Trades Unions, business men, manufacturers and others. Even the aristocratic classes have been liquidated and resentment and hatred must burn like a seething fire beneath an outwardly calm exterior. At the moment all Germany is in the hysterical position of visualizing unlimited success, the triumph of the *herrenrasse*, but at the first sign of real disaster the neuroticism, the inner turmoil, the wild fears and hatreds of these people, will boil to the surface. Air operations properly conceived and used, can pry the lid off of this Pandora's box.

Once psychological deterioration sets in within a highly organized industrial society its strength as a cohesive unit is finished. A whole city can be taken under these circumstances even though the army be intact, as when the little minority of the Bolsheviki took over Leningrad in 1917, or when a mere handful of intellectual Young Turks seized the government at Constantinople against the apathetic Sultan and his retinue. It is well within the memory of the German Government that a few Nazi radicals came within an ace of capturing Austria after the assassination of Chancellor Dollfuss, and actually did hold the reins of power for several hours.

There is a very reasonable possibility of a savagely vindictive fifth column group rising out of the residue of pre-Nazi Germany, which could be relied upon as a co-operating element. The Battle of Crete furnishes a prototype for the operations which could be involved in mopping up the remnants of resistance and occupying this territory, once the enemy has been disabled and his will to continue demoralized. An operation which envisaged the landing of half a million or even a million men under these conditions, would be easily within the power of our armed forces. This expeditionary force would not be primarily an army of invasion but one of occupation. It would not fight its way in from bridgeheads on the coasts but would be landed in the very center of the country, basing itself on airports and other strategic centers.

This entire plan of procedure presupposes that a general command of the air over Germany will not be attained until the very end, and that attacks would be in the nature of forays involving temporary rule of the skies over localized areas.

This estimate of the situation undoubtedly errs on the side of conservatism. Certainly if absolute command of the skies over Germany can once be established all schemes of maneuver become pale and superfluous. The situation would, under those circumstances, be completely dominated by naked air power in the hands of the Allied generals. German installations of every kind could be reduced at leisure. The Third Reich would then be doomed.

IV

The Far Eastern theater can hardly be looked on as a sideshow. The Japs are formidable and tough opponents, and even with the fall of Germany will remain there still to be beaten. Nevertheless, the strategical requirements operate against the splitting of our forces. We are not strong enough to beat both the Axis partners at one time and are compelled to take them on in detail.

As far as Japan is concerned, there are three principal points from which we could strike now. One is Hawaii which is 3882 miles from Tokio and which, incidentally, General Mitchell considered relatively subordinate to the circle of islands which bisects the Bering Strait and connects Alaska with the Asian mainland. If we can equip and hold a base at Dutch Harbor and build a good military road from the continental United States to the key Alaskan bases, we will be only 2174 miles from the tip of the main Japanese island. Our lines of communication for any other form of attack are absolutely impossible, due to their length alone.

The most favorable base would be Vladivostok which is only 665 miles from Tokio, but there is no tenable hope of retaining it once the Japanese were conscious of the fact that it was to be used as a springboard for an offensive against their principal cities.

Probably the most that can be said for an offensive against the Japanese islands at this time is its moral effect and its deterring influence on Nipponese operations elsewhere. Such a strategy could only be justified if it succeeded in having the psychological effect of placing the Japanese on the defensive. From a purely military view it would seem that the providential conjunction of factors makes Germany the objective in the first concentration of assault. She is at once accessible to attack and is, moreover, the strongest, hence the principal enemy.

Just as we seriously underrated them before, we now with equal lack of reason consider the Japanese military as a practically irresistible fighting force. Actually the Japanese have yet to prove their mettle against a first-class fighting army under terms which approach equality of armament and position. Wherever they have gone, they have won by virtue of crushing numbers and overwhelming superiority of planes and other fighting machines.

Despite their fantastic exploits in sinking capital ships, they are especially weak in the air. Wherever they have met our boys on equal terms, as at Bataan, over the Coral Sea, or in the Battle of Midway, Japanese fliers have been badly worsted.

The Nipponese air force is a miscellany of slavishly imitated American and German types. The Japs have originated little in reference to airplane and engine construction. They would be left far behind if technical improvements were to be suddenly developed in America. Kawanishi, for example, builds short seaplanes with Rolls-Royce motors. Kawasaki makes pursuit planes and bombers with licenses from Dornier and BMW. Mitsubishi constructs Curtiss pursuits and Junkers dive-bombers with Hispano-Suiza and Junkers motors, while Nakajima has licenses from Douglas and Fokker, and for Lorraine and Bristol motors. It may be said without fear of error that practically all Japanese craft are adaptations of models which are at least a year or two behind the current types in the countries which originally developed them. Even the vaunted

Zero fighter is a composite of American and British types, lightened for increased climbing speed.

It is doubtful whether the Japs are turning out 8000 military airplanes a year. Though they have picked up a great amount of aluminum in Manchuria and the East Indies, they are seriously short of machine tools and other vital appurtenances to this industry.

Today the Nipponese are operating over a battle-ground in eastern and southeastern Asia and the great archipelago of more than 27,000,000 square miles. The Island Empire is forced to scatter its limited supply of aircraft over a wide area. Once the elements of surprise and decisive massings are eliminated, Japan is forced to think in terms of protecting the immense territory it has acquired. This means defensive operations over an extended area and the dispersal of its aeronautical strength. There must be important squadrons in Manchuria, in China, in Burma, and certainly through the South Seas. Once the Japanese run up against a first-class land-based air power which is in a position to take the initiative and strike from well-prepared bases, their whole military position will rapidly disintegrate.

As a land and sea power Nippon is powerful enough to stand siege for the entire predictable future. She has a well-equipped and finely trained army of almost 7,000,000 men, only a small portion of which is actually engaged on the battle lines of Asia.

Japan's geographical position as a naval power would render any attack by water practically suicidal. According to Bywater, she "could build each year four capital ships . . . four to six light cruisers and twenty to twenty-five destroyers and fourteen to twenty submarines." [30] Her ability to do so in case of need is beyond question. To her rear are the Japan and Yellow Seas, which wash on Korea and Manchukuo and the occupied ports of China. She holds fast every island stepping-stone which would be required to launch an attack against her home centers, and is reaching out for strategic bastions into the Indian Ocean.

Any effort aimed at taking Japan from the sea is a chimera. She can only be successfully assaulted from the land flank, and this involves active Chinese participation and probably that of the Soviets as well.

The key to domination of the Pacific Ocean is Alaska with its connecting necklace of islands forming an air-power bridge around the neck of water which separates the land mass of the Old World from the New. These constitute a great highway pointing directly at the big Russian air and submarine base of Vladivostok, which is, itself, only an hour and a half as the crow flies, from Tokio. The main American base is at Dutch Harbor which is only 1400 miles away from the big Siberian peninsula of Kamchatka, with the many stepping-stones of the Aleutian Islands in between. This great tongue of Soviet territory cuts directly across the supply lines leading from the Aleutians to the south; hence no attack can be made upon Alaska which does not at the same time involve an attack on eastern Siberia.

If we strongly fortify the mainland of Alaska as well

[30] *Sea Power in the Pacific*, p. 176.

as the chain of islands curving off from it to the west, protecting these natural fortresses with an interlacing network of powerful air bases, we may safely utilize a holding action against Japan while engaged in the job of subduing Germany. Once the Reich is out of the war, Russia and allied portions of Europe would be able to throw their entire effort into a crushing attack on the Nipponese Empire. We ourselves could then land men and machines over a safe land route. A large-scale land operation in Asia would knock Japan into a cocked hat, and her defeat on the mainland would doom her islands to extinction. Her industries would be instantly deprived of major sources of coal, manganese and animal and vegetable products she badly requires. The open door to a land invasion is provided by the rolling prairies of Mongolia and Manchuria which favor the use of mechanized equipment.

The Land of the Rising Sun would discover itself in the sad position of fighting alone against virtually the balance of the universe.

Air power attacks would find all of her cities tragically vulnerable. Air raid shelters are highly inadequate and the towns themselves are as inflammable as so many match boxes. An assault on water reservoirs, or on a few hydraulic and thermal generating plants, would pile up the metropolis of Tokio in hopeless confusion.

Most of the railways are electrified and can be put out of commission by bombing the one main track with its transformers and transmission lines. The hub of the railroad system is Tokio whose orderly existence would be turned into bedlam if the yards were destroyed. The blowing up of a single railroad bridge would do the trick alone. The three vehicular bridges which span the wide muddy Shinagawa are the sole arteries connecting Tokio and the north with busy Yokohama and its automotive, chemical, and electrical manufacturing plants.

Japan's chief manufacturing centers are situated on the islands of Honshu, Hokkaido, Shikoku, and Kyushu. The great matrix of her industrial life is an area forty miles through the middle, reaching in a long strip from Tokio to Shimonoseki, and from there a short jump across the water to Kyushu, where sixty per cent of the Island Kingdom's iron and steel tonnage is produced. In this concentrated belt, a target as attractive as the German Ruhr, are dockyards, munitions manufactories, steel mills, metal and engineering shops, and heavy industry of all kinds. In the north of Honshu are the great hydraulic electric plants which produce over eighty per cent of the country's electric power, which is so centralized as to provide one of the most inviting targets for demolition bombing in existence.

A sea blockade against Japan, similar to the one undertaken by Germany against England, would greatly weaken the Nipponese and perhaps throttle them completely. The long Japanese supply line is a trilateral affair reaching from the Solomon Islands and the Indian Ocean to the point of Kyushu. By cutting through this funnel, either between Luzon and Formosa, or between Formosa and Kyushu, the Japanese war machine would be seriously hurt and Nippon would face imminent starvation.

Japan is more exposed to this type of attack than any other nation. Immense gaps of water separate her from all her outposts and sources of supply. It is 3595 miles from Tokio to Batavia, and an equal distance to New Guinea and the islands of the Coral Sea. To Rangoon and the Burma front is 3000 miles.

The rocky Japanese islands are crowded with more than 70,000,000 people, the greatest population density of any of the large nations. The Island Kingdom must import at least 10,000,000 tons of vital raw materials a year if its industry is to be kept going. This would involve some 2,000,000 gross tons of shipping to supply her barest minimum requirements. At the start of the war Japan is said to have possessed around 5,000,-000 gross tons of shipping. Of this it has already lost an estimated twenty per cent. With all her known yards working, Nippon cannot turn out more than 900,000 tons of merchant shipping a year. Should the United Nations sink only 200,000 tons a month, Japan's bridge of ships would soon break.[31]

American submarines have already been busy hacking away at the Japanese lifeline with excellent results. By mid-April 1942, American forces had sunk or crippled more than 160 Japanese ships—a rate of better than one a day.

There is no reason in the world why we should not outbuild the Axis in submarines. At the present time we possess quite a substantial undersea fleet. One hundred and twelve are actually in operation, with an-

[31] According to British records, the Germans frequently sank more than 500,000 tons of Allied shipping a month.

other fifteen or twenty in various stages of construction. There are perhaps some seventy on blueprints.

If this is the means by which we can cut the throat of the Japanese cyclops, nothing should prevent us from building 500 or even 1000 submarines. American technological genius and facilities can turn them into a weapon far more formidable than the Germans ever conceived.

Like the airplane, the submarine is still in the experimental stage and presents possibilities for great accomplishments. It may be possible to build them of gigantic size. The big French boat, *Surcouf*, carried a scout plane in the hangar on its deck and was equipped with two eight-inch guns and two 37-millimeter guns, as well as her regular tubes and a nest of machine guns, making it a truly formidable weapon. The improvements to be looked for are an increase in the number of torpedoes and tubes, as well as a greatly extended cruising radius and carrying capacity. The addition of strength to the hull plating and frame will ultimately allow a depth test of as much as 600 feet, making the raider completely invisible to scouting aircraft.

It has even been advanced that the submarine be considered as a cargo carrier. A 3000-ton underwater boat, by sacrificing torpedo space, could carry 200 men across the ocean. Twenty such ships plus thirty others carrying four amphibian tanks apiece, would provide the elements of occupying power on any weakly-held shore.

A daring project which may already have been put into execution by the Japanese, explaining the presence of their little two-man submarines in Pearl Harbor, stemmed from the experiments of the British submarine commander, Colin Mayers.[32] This brilliant inventor advocated the construction of large mother submarines with long cruising radii. Smaller subs carried within the mother's belly, could be released under water at full speed and engage the enemy shipping in packs. Complete blueprints were made with specially constructed runways down which small submarines "no larger than a whale" would slide in cradles, liberating themselves about twenty feet below the surface.[33] The plan was never carried out by the British Admiralty which regarded it as "fantastic."

Colin Mayers built several experimental models of an artillery submarine carrying a 12-inch cannon fore of the conning tower, with the gun-housing watertight so as to enable the crew to load and service the weapon while submerged. It was anticipated that this powerful arm would be able to deliver its shells six seconds after the submarine had broken surface. Mayers also advocated sub-sea aircraft carriers with hydraulically operated hangar doors, enabling the planes to get in quickly so that submergence could proceed without delay. "In the art of submarine-aircraft co-operation on the high seas as well as for coastal operations," he wrote with dramatic vision, "we are just on the threshold of many interesting developments."

[32] It may be assumed that Colin Mayers' idea was developed by the Japanese, who are known to have searched the patent files for information about small submarines.

[33] Colin Mayers, *Submarines, Admirals, and Navies*, 1940.

V

One of the main problems involved in an intensive campaign by air against the Germans is that of transportation, particularly as it concerns the question of an assured fuel supply. A Flying Fortress may consume more than 10,000 gallons of oil in twenty-four hours. A fleet of 1000 planes of all required types might involve a fuel expenditure up to 12,000 tons for a single night's operations.

In an attempt to annul this contemplated action at its source, the Nazi Command has converged its efforts on cutting the arteries through which the supply of aviation gasoline flows to England. In our coastal zone alone we have been losing some eight oil tankers a month,[34] a damage we can ill afford. In the first six months of 1942, a total of 275 ships were sunk in American waters—a circumstance to which we can hardly remain indifferent. Many other types of goods, in addition to ore, must be shipped, not only to China and to Russia to keep them in the war, but in particular to our pivotal base in the North Sea, Britain, without which this conflict cannot be won by us.

The Germans are known to be bending every effort on the production of torpedo-carrying aircraft as well as U-boats, which can suddenly be released in a pack to isolate Britain by slashing its supply lines. The grave danger, as has been suggested, is that the present depre-

[34] This is based on the period before March 11. No additional information has been since released.

dations, serious as they are, do not represent the peak of Axis striking power, and are instead experimental forays intended as a proving ground for future tactics, and that a massive assault is in preparation with the object of completely wiping out our trans-Atlantic shipping in a single paralyzing stroke.

There are no more important zones of defense than the wide avenues of sea which lead to our external sources of raw materials and to the far-flung island fortresses around which our outer barricades are woven. The battle against the submarine remains precarious. Our method of meeting it is simply to build boats and cargoes at a rate faster than the Axis is able to send them to the bottom of the sea.

If the entire question were one of successful convoy, the use of patrol planes in great numbers would greatly relieve the situation. Convoying aircraft force U-boats to travel submerged and hence at low speed, thus drastically reducing their range of operations.

The submarine knows that it can be seen with comparative ease from above, and common prudence forces it to break contact with the convoyed ships and keep itself at a safe distance. It is aware that once it is spotted, any depth charge dropped in its vicinity will have its name on it. The British even used inoffensive little pleasure craft like the Tiger Moth, during the critical days after Dunkerque to prowl over the coastal waters—a bold piece of bluff which had an extraordinary effect in keeping the deadly pig boats at a distance.

As a supplement to the work of long-range machines such as the Consolidated B-24 or Catalina PB-2Y-2, it is entirely possible to make provision in merchant-ship construction for small torpedo planes or light bombers. These could take off from ship decks under control of certain inexpensive apparatus which has already been proposed; or they could be thrown into the air by catapults, a method which is beginning to be widely used. If patroling machines were used in sufficient quantities the coastal waters on both sides of the Atlantic to a depth of at least 500 miles, could be kept clear of raiders.

But such an effort is, at best, makeshift. It is in the history of all protective devices that they palliate but never cure. Ways and means are found to meet them, and relative success must be measured by the degree of expense and trouble required to make the relief effective.

A better method would be to cancel out this situation altogether by removing our cargo ships from the surface of the seas, shifting by calculated transition stages to a merchant marine on wings.

Those of us who have watched the tremendous evolutionary processes taking place in the business of transport as well as in the art of war, are convinced that this question cannot be settled until we have abandoned our orthodox methods of conveyance in favor of a radical all-out control by aircraft.

The day is swiftly coming, and it is here now if we so will it, when all important long distance hauling will be done by airplanes, enormous craft stripped to mere skin and motors for the purpose of carrying heavy freight. We need no longer be tied to the

Burma Road, to the gray surface of the Atlantic or to the icelocked northwest passage to Russia. If we can forego our orthodox devotion to traditional methods we can give ourselves in the field of supply as well as battle, that capacity for swift movement which characterizes the successful campaigns of this era.

When the time element is reckoned in together with the cost of construction and ratio of loss by sinkings, it would be *cheaper now* to open our transoceanic supply lines by air, rather than attempt to meet the challenge of the submarine by an increased production of sinkable surface ships.

It is we alone who have the machinery, the industrial capacity and the resources to attempt this. With one cut of the sword we can slash the Gordian knot which ties us to these myriad and manifold problems of transportation and of supply. We can bring in chromite from Mexico and tungsten from China, and we can send men and machinery to whatever point of this globe we decide, exclusively by air.

We can today, if we wish, build great fleets of glider cargo carriers, which can be hitched behind towing airplanes and cross either ocean with safety, economy, and efficiency. The army expert, Lewin Barringer, sees long-range traction-planes designed and built for this specific purpose, carrying crew, radio and fuel, with all passengers and freight, moving along at 200 miles per hour in the trailing gliders. The advent of plastic gliders makes it possible to think in terms of ten- and twelve-ton cargo-carrying gliders towed in line. Plastic gliders could be slapped out in astronomical numbers in comparison with the production speed of the fabric-covered tubing type used today.[35]

The flying cargo carrier could be built of plywood, steel, laminated plastic or other substances not on the critical list. Yards and shops now devoted to shipbuilding and allied types of construction, could easily be adjusted to the manufacture of freight planes and parts.

In addition to providing the required insurance against a surprise German action, aerial transport might even prove cheaper than that in use now. Among factors which must be considered in addition to original investment are cost of operation per cargo-pound, expense of convoys, and loss of merchandise by sinkings.

The aerial carrier could operate on low octane gas or Diesel fuel, and would be powered with relatively inexpensive engines capable of taking hard punishment, rather than of speed. Five hundred or more miles from their ports of destination they could be met by escorting fighters.

In 1937 a report made by the United States Maritime Commission already recognized that "the addition of aircraft to the fleets of shipping companies now seems to be justified. . . . The cost of passenger transportation over the ocean is likely to be less on future aircraft than on superliners. This conclusion is arrived at by a comparison of the cost of depreciation, fuel, and crew for the superliner and both types of

[35] J. G. Underhill, "Axis Air Transport," *Infantry Journal*, issue of February 1942.

aircraft—the flying boat and the dirigible. Aircraft designs now available for immediate construction *would enable a fleet of eighteen flying boats, on a daily service of three planes a day, to offer the same total passenger capacity for a year as the superliner, at a production cost for building the planes estimated at $18,000,000 against an American production of $50,000,000 for the superliner.*[36]

"The superliner," comments the report briefly, "requires four or five times as many horsepower-hours per passenger as does the flying boat . . . the relatively low costs indicated for trans-oceanic flying are remarkable, as it is extremely rare in the history of transport development of any kind that the faster passenger service proves in its early stages to be the cheapest." [37]

Grover Loening points out that it takes nearly two months for the average ten-mile-an-hour convoyed freighter to travel the 12,000 miles from our East Coast around the tip of Africa to the Red Sea or the Persian Gulf. He figures that the type of flying ship now in our possession can carry a useful load, on such a run, of twenty tons. A plane of this type could easily make seventy trips a year across the Atlantic, delivering 140,000 tons of cargo.[38] Without dipping heavily into our reserve of essential materials, we could turn out 1000 such aircraft a month.

This is a war in which the supply lines will have

[36] Italics are the author's.
[37] *Economic Survey of the American Merchant Marine*, pp. 23-25, United States Maritime Commission, November 19, 1937.
[38] "Ships Over the Sea," April 1942 issue of *Foreign Affairs*.

the last say. In this first true conflict on a global scale a premium is paid on mobility—on the capacity to "get there fustest with the mostest." [39] If we could pour aid in to Chiang Kai-shek, completely emancipated from reliance on railroads and crawling mountain arteries, we could erect a major front against the Japanese, facing them with millions of resolute well-armed Chinamen. We could fly our regiments, tanks and guns over the short North Pole route to Russia without the slightest danger of interference.

With this supplying air train we could move great armies of goods and men to any threatened point, to the Panama Canal, to the Caribbean islands, to Alaska, or to South America. We could terminate the battle of the Atlantic, taking our cargo carriers out of the reach of raiders, and could seize command of circumglobular transportation.

For years the heaviest freight has been delivered cheaply and efficiently by cargo planes in the countries bordering the Andes, in Honduras, and in our wild northwest. The Nazis turned the entire course of history by ferrying Franco's crack Moorish Army across from Morocco in their Ju-52's at a time when the Fascist revolt seemed doomed. These planes brought 4000 men and 200 tons of war freight to the relief of Seville alone.

Crete was an example of a fully-developed air ferry in operation. So was the supplying of General Rommel's depleted *Afrika Korps*, enabling him to throw the astonished British Army of the Nile back on its

[39] General Forrest's famous dictum.

heels in eastern Libya. The Italian Savoia Marchetti SM-82 not only has been carting equipment and men but has also been carrying fighting planes. It is quite capable of ferrying a single-seat fighter such as the Macchi C-200, across the Mediterranean. "Five hundred JU-52 transports," comments Underhill, "could move a United States triangular division from Crete to Libya in less than twenty-four hours. From June 22 to the beginning of August, German transport squadrons—probably equipped with fifteen JU-52's—moved about 6,000,000 pounds of supplies to the Russian front and carried 2381 wounded back to hospitals." [40]

The Germans have been well ahead of us in the development of this spectacular innovation in long-distance transport. The United States Army, however, has been quietly developing its own system of aerial transport linking up its big supply depots at Middletown, Pennsylvania, San Antonio, Texas, and San Francisco, California. It now handles a greater tonnage of air freight than all other agencies of the Western Hemisphere combined. An increasing stock of essential military goods is now being flown over the high wall of the Himalayas into China by U. S. Army pilots. It is estimated that by autumn a greater weight of supplies can be delivered weekly by air carriers of a type now in production, than the full capacity of 8000 trucks painfully creeping over the hairpin turns of the now-defunct Burma Road.

Our army now possesses various types of military

[40] "Axis Air Transport," *Infantry Journal*, February 1942 issue.

carriers which are capable of carrying from fifty to a hundred fully armed infantrymen along with their equipment. These planes which could cross the Atlantic with ease, fully loaded, will soon come off the assembly lines in impressive numbers. One of these is the Lockheed Constellation, with a cruising speed of 250 miles per hour and a comfortable ceiling of 30,000 feet. Another is the 25-ton Curtiss Condor III, a machine efficient enough to compete commercially at Railway Express rates for long hauls.

If the U. S. Government were deliberately to set itself to the problem of producing heavy, powerful sky freighters, loads comparable to those now being transported by slow surface vessels could be easily carried. Glenn Martin visualizes great fleets of commercial transport planes weighing up to 500,000 pounds. Grover Loening considers entirely practical a machine which would have twelve engines of 3000 horsepower each. Such engines, in fact, have already been designed. "Loaded with twenty-five pounds to the horsepower . . . this 36,000 horsepower plane will take into the air a total of 900,000 pounds or 450 tons. . . . Its load-carrying capacity would be somewhere around 350,000 pounds or 175 tons." [41] This giant would deliver approximately 12,000 tons a year to an area as far away as the Red Sea.

Once attention were centered on this problem, many methods could be contrived to increase load-carrying capacity of all types. Assisted take-off is one which promises great possibilities for the immediate future. Refueling by air is another.

[41] "Ships Over the Sea," *Foreign Affairs*, April 1942 issue.

There are also real possibilities for the rigid airships as trans-oceanic freighters. General Billy Mitchell believed they could be made valuable as mother ships for airplanes as well as fuel carriers.[42] A rigid airship of 10,000,000 cubic foot capacity, says Admiral William C. Pratt, could carry ten attack bombers "with an efficiency perhaps twenty-five per cent greater than similar types used on aircraft carriers, at a range of 10,000 miles and a speed of fifty knots." Such a carrier could transport several hundred tons of useful load over the Atlantic, flying high above the cloud banks.[43] Or they could carry fifty fighter planes from New York across the ocean in not more than forty-eight hours.

Provision would have to be made to convoy such ships when they came within the known range of hostile airplanes, though if they were to travel in flotillas one might be constituted as an aircraft carrier and the others merely as cargo transports, thus making themselves self-sufficient as a protective unit.

The creation of a vast air carrier organization would relieve the big ships of the Navy from convoy work, allowing them to resume other functions for which they are fitted. It would furnish us with a secure, flexible supply line together with an invaluable body of trained pilots, mechanics, meteorologists and radio operators. It would give this country immediate com-

[42] Testimony before Joint Committee to Investigate Dirigible Disasters, Seventy-third Congress, First Session, June 1, 1933.

[43] The United States is the only known source of helium gas with which the big bags are inflated. See also *Economic Survey of the American Merchant Marine*, United States Maritime Commission, November 19, 1937.

mand of circumglobular transportation and with it a mobility and freedom of operation unmatched by the farthest stretch of the military imagination.

VI

The difficulty and cost of preparing a program of this magnitude cannot be denied. But recall the difficulty and the cost of implementing any part of the vast rearmament program now in preparation! There is certainly nothing minor in the effort to create a mass army of 8,000,000 men fully equipped and mechanized, nor in the great shipbuilding project, nor in the construction program for aviation to be used auxiliary to the ground forces. The whole business simply comes down to one of measuring tasks and determining where, with the time equation in view, the greatest value can be secured.

The proposed air offensive is intended to carry the main burden of the war effort, with all other forces playing largely contributory roles. While in absolute quantities the scale of the contemplated attack may seem prohibitive, compared to other forms of armed operations it is really moderate. Consider the fact that German artillery on the Eastern front probably uses 250,000 rounds a day—1250 tons in dead weight. To this must be added the ammunition used by the Wehrmacht of .50 caliber and smaller, in machine guns, sub-machine guns, automatic rifles and sidearms, which amounts to some 2,000,000 rounds a day; and of trench mortars, rifle mortars, hand grenades and land mines—some 450,000 units per day averaging about two pounds each.

At the battle of St. Mihiel more than 1,000,000 shells, averaging at least fifteen pounds each, were fired in four hours. In the Meuse-Argonne Battle, 2417 guns were used and approximately 4,214,000 rounds of artillery fired. The daily cost of war materials in World War I was $10,000,000. Seventy-five tons of metal plus twenty-five tons of powder were shipped for each German killed or wounded.

An aerial assault of this magnitude would be only a matter of a few brief months at the most, whereas ground campaigns involving colossal armies of clashing men and machines may continue at the same steady grueling gait for years. The investment of lives, too, would be minor compared to the shocking losses which would inevitably eventuate from any attempted frontal attack on land.

If we disperse all our resources in a vast Lend-Lease program it must be recognized that these resources no longer belong to us, nor does the experience of handling them in battle belong to us. Just as Thailand turned the airplanes granted them under Lend-Lease against the United Nations after Japan took over, so any nation may do so. To play the role of the fat banker is not conducive to victory. We should seek as far as possible to man our own machines and to implement our attack power by our own fighters. Neither money, obligation nor gratitude is ever a substitute for a well-armed, experienced body of fighting men in guaranteeing the future peace.

With an air force of shattering strength at our

command, we will have complete control over the military situation over the entire earth, preventing for all time, if it is our purpose to do so, the re-emergence of such a vicious excrescence as Nazi Germany or Hirohito's Japan. Otherwise it is essentially possible that the winning of this war would simply be the prelude to new wars in the usual cycle of historical changes.

As another factor of at least passing interest, when the time comes and this bloody contest is finally over, it will be the air installations alone which will have any value in the post-war period of reconstruction which is to follow. All other war production will have to be junked, contributing little, if anything, to the future well-being of our people.

To implement an aircraft development project of these dimensions, a rigidly enforced first priority must be given to the air program, whether it concerns strategic raw materials, factory space, electric power, or manpower.

Until the middle of last February, the only war equipment enjoying the highest priority rating (A-1-a) was battleships. Other naval construction, plus tanks, trucks and related equipment rated next. Four-engine bombers had an A-1-b rating, and all other types of combat planes were down at A-1-d. Aircraft engines, without which planes are useless, were on the list at A-1-d. Public opinion then forced a revision which put aircraft on a par with battleships in a so-called fluid relationship.

Despite the A-1-a rating on tools for heavy bombers,

other portions of the national defense have succeeded in securing even more urgent priorities, leaving air-craft builders without required machinery. "Boeing, for example, in desperate need of four additional mechanical presses, has been unable to get delivery quotations earlier than March for the first half and May for the second. It has been trying without suc-cess to persuade the War Department to release sev-eral such machines from shell plants." [44] The situation is equally critical for engine manufacturers, many of whom may be half a year behind in deliveries unless some strong arm with a machete at the end of it, man-ages to slash through this swathing of insistent priori-ties granted to the Army and Navy for other construc-tion purposes.

The shortage of materials has become so acute that aviation factories have lost many of their vital sub-contractors to producers of other weapons. The air-craft program which began on a three-shift production schedule, had to fall back in February to one and a half shifts. Meanwhile aluminum and other "deficit" materials essential to the manufacture of heavy bomb-ers, are still being absorbed by other types of war pro-duction. For example, $8000 worth of fudge-warmers were ordered by the Army recently, to be made out of aluminum.[45] The Army still specifies copper roof gutters, roofs, and downspouts. In minesweepers and PT boats the requirements are for all-copper water-pipes, though in ordinary yachts pipes are usually of galvanized iron. The galleys on both PT boats and

[44] *Fortune* Magazine, October 1941.
[45] This order was finally canceled on the priority route.

minesweepers are finished entirely in the very scarce monel metal.

Only the general recognition that an air offensive holds the key to victory can force a genuine channeling of materials and energies to aircraft production. Once air power has the acknowledged right of way, there is no limit to the production miracles which can be achieved.

We require a strict rationing of all raw materials on which there may be a scarcity, so as to create stock piles on which the aircraft industry will have unchallenged priority. No material out of which a bombing plane could be built should then be devoted to any other purposes, except those which contribute directly to the upkeep and maintenance of the air fleet. Starting at that point where limitation of essential material places a stop order on the expansion of plane-building, such construction as aircraft carriers, submarines, tanks, armored cars and small, fast boats of the fleet could go forward.

Since there is a definite limitation to the amount of aluminum,[46] magnesium, and other critical metals which can be used in a plane-building program, the heavy bomber industry should have first call, with fighter planes achieving a moderate ratio. All others, including freight carriers and trainers, should be made

---

[46] According to an item in the *Wall Street Journal*, Henry Ford and the Union Carbide and Carbon Corporation expect to produce between them, under a new process, more than 70,000,000 pounds of magnesium a year. It is hoped, too, that the American genius for production will enable us to turn out the unheard of total of 2,000,-000,000 pounds of aluminum per annum by making use of native North American resources.

out of substitute materials. One of these is steel, which may be used wherever increased weight and lessened speed are not serious shortcomings. Another is plywood, the material out of which planes were universally constructed up until fifteen years ago. One of the newest and best British service types is made entirely of plywood, and the Italians have at least four bombers made of the same stuff. The most numerous fighter type owned by the Soviets is of all-plywood tail and wing construction. Only at points requiring extreme strength will metal be used in the new aircraft designs.

Skins of laminated plastic can be at least three times as thick as those of duralumin, without exceeding the latter's weight. This thickness and greater stiffness make less reinforcement necessary. Since rivets and overlaps are not required, a plywood fighter with a power plant identical with that used by a metal fighter, will have a slight edge in speed—perhaps as much as twenty-five miles an hour.

Parts made of these materials are easy to machine and are often functionally superior. The fuselage for a Canadian Avro-Anson bomber built by Vidal Research Corporation, in recent static tests is shown to be fifteen per cent lighter than metal and fabric models and capable of sustaining heavier loads.[47] Wherever corrosion is an important factor, plywood has the additional quality of being moisture-resistant.

There is much less time taken in construction than in metal types. According to Dr. Maurice H. Bigelow, a plywood plane could be produced in one-tenth the

[47] Herbert Chase, *Aviation Industry*, May 15, 1941.

time and at a fraction of the cost of an aluminum plane of the same size.

There is absolutely no limit to the amount of resources available in factory space, human skill and basic materials when it comes to making plywood ships. These planes can be turned out on a real mass production basis, utilizing woodworking machinery now idle. Parts can be built in the plants of furniture manufacturers, piano factories, or small boat builders, whose supporting industries have practically shut down for the duration.

A wartime measure which would be entirely justified would be the seizure of the untold tons of aluminum and other essential metals which are to be found in homes and restaurants throughout the country. There must be upwards of 50,000,000 pounds in cooking utensils alone. These would serve to relieve the demands on our stock piles from other sources. There is nothing more abhorrent in this invasion of the kitchen and this conscription of metallic possessions, than there is in the conscription of humans. In England they are even melting down historic iron fences in the national interest, and where these are not willingly given they are seized.

It is interesting to note that under stress Britain has learned to economize, to cut the waste due to premature junking and to extend the life of parts far beyond that now conceived in this country. There are some twenty shops which specialize in reclamation work on engines alone.

Every plan for reclamation is subject to exhaustive tests and thoroughly explored. They weld, cast, calibrate, and grind cracked and worn parts. When the writer was there they were even attempting to reclaim bowed crankshafts. There are almost no throwaways. Like the pig in the stockyards, all is used but the squeak.

All parts, housings, etc., are individually tested for leaks and flaws—not just reassembled. The engine is gone over in relation to its logbook, as if it were some living patient. It is torn down altogether after 240 hours for the fighter and 360 for the bomber.

On all crack-ups added together there is only an average four per cent junking.

The manager of this hospital for sick engines told the author: "The time will come when America will overhaul three engines for each one built." A successful program of this kind has almost exactly the same effect as if it were an added percentage of new production.

To operate this ambitious construction plan would require a minimum of some 5,000,000 workers. The War Department's little-known Civilian Defense Training Program could produce practically all of the mechanics needed on short notice. Under no circumstance should toolmakers, mechanics, or other workers who could be turned to the business of producing aircraft, be put into the armed forces. The aircraft industry should have first claim on all of these, and the mere fact of employment in this industry or any trade related to it, should constitute exemption in itself.

Every plant which could possibly be adapted to this purpose should be put to work. There are thousands of parts to airplanes, and if necessary, little artisan shops and backyard garages could be set to fabricating these. There are many factories capable of manufacturing military aircraft or parts, which have been unable to secure any substantial place for themselves in the expansion program, causing a great number of small machine shops and skilled laborers to be idle.

According to the Truman report, there exists an "ingrained distrust of small companies, a lack of knowledge of their facilities, and reluctance to place greater supervisory load on already overworked Army and Navy personnel." We should alter this wasteful system, or at least set up a supplementary production method which will parallel it. We cannot extract the last drop of juice from the industrial orange unless there is a co-ordination of all plants and factories, large or small, capable of rendering a wartime service.

We could also speed our production upward on a sharply rising arc by calling a halt to the inordinate number of changes which are continually made in design. Once the prototype has been approved, there should be no further alterations. The vast dangers of this procedure are painfully illustrated by the record left by the French Air Ministry. The ceaseless changes in pattern it ordered so interfered with the process of manufacture that production dwindled to a minor trickle.

Yet in order to achieve massive output it is necessary to freeze a good part of our designs. This would mean two separate types of thinking—one engaged in stabilizing types for production, and another concerned with a constant stream of alterations for experimental purposes, so that there could be an essential compromise between the two ideas. The experience of the Germans against the better equipped English during the Battle for Britain, shows the danger of wholesale standardization even for the sake of quantity output.

The whole question becomes one of procurement methods, of that genius for management and efficiency which has allowed the American people to out-produce, out-design, and out-sell the world during the past century.

VII. ORGANIZATION FOR WAR

TO accomplish this program and implement it quickly, Air Power must be recognized as the single weapon by which domination may be achieved, and all tactics should be directly designed around it. The principal armed strength of the country would be in airplanes, with all war-making elements organized as more or less autonomous sections of a single unit. Wars can no longer be successfully fought by fractional elements operating under independent leadership, but only by completely synchronized attack bodies. The geographical and strategic conditions under which this war is to be fought, together with the logistics involved, automatically delivers leadership to Air Power, with the existing surface forces assigned to auxiliary roles.

We would discard, then, our present conception of a great mass army in favor of a compact professional army of not more than 2,000,000 men, equipped and trained for the task of moving in after seizure of the air spaces over the enemy's territory has rendered further resistance on his part hopeless. The Army would be an administrative and policing body, built in part on the new commando principle, capable of extensive mopping-up operations and of complete administration of any territory under its control. It would understand the handling of industry, the management of technological resources, and the problems relating to the control of conquered populations. This compact mass of professional fighters and administrators would be altogether on wheels and caterpillar treads, so as to give it the greatest possible effectiveness in mobility and concentrated firepower.

The Navy, constructed with the view to being assistant to this all-out aerial attack, would consist of rapidly evolved types of aircraft carriers and a growing underseas fleet. In the largest sense it, too, would be basically an aerial organization. It would become a giant transport organization devoted to the peculiar problems of keeping the sea roads clear, of organizing and protecting the all-important supply lines. Its function of the initiative would disappear except as it related to submarine and aerial attacks on enemy shipping. As the great schools of tankers, merchant and troop ships which we are moving over the waters of the globe are gradually replaced by air cargo trains, the big surface battle-wagons will pass through the same transitionary stage as did the wooden frigates of the last century.

The entire machinery of procurement and combat as it relates to the air should be thrown into one, with direct representation in the President's cabinet. All research, experimentation, development and procurement work should be pooled in a subsidiary Department of Aircraft Production. There should be a single system of factory inspection, one standard for fuels and lubricants, and a unification of airport control.

Training programs including that for paratroops and air infantry would come under a single related Bureau.

The usual argument advanced against an integral air force is that the act of separation would cause the Army and Navy to lose control over one of the most essential sections in their whole structure of command. There is a quite understandable reluctance on the part of the older services to relinquish any part of their existing establishments. Every corps and fleet commander feels the need for close air protection of his own units and naturally clamors for squadrons directly under his jurisdiction. "That tendency," comments Viscount Trenchard, "unless rigidly resisted can only end in disaster. . . . It hardly needed Pearl Harbor to prove that the air defense of a fleet base or of an area of land operations is not a naval or an army function."

The question is fundamentally one of view and of strategic purpose. Even if the Air Force were directed by a brilliant, non-flying general, it is fundamental to its organization that it be *primarily designed as an air force, not as an adjunct to the operations of surface forces.* No officer who has been trained in the function of destroying an opposing army can conceive of bombing operations in the rear aimed exclusively at disrupting the enemy's communications or morale. A man who thinks in terms of 200 miles as a difficult and complicated day's journey for an armored infantry on wheels, cannot possibly visualize round-trip operations of 2000 miles in a single day in which no question of "occupying power" or destruction of fortified places enters.

A certain amount of compromise could be advantageously employed and the Army could retain its own limited air services for tactical reconnaissance, photography and dive-bombing, wherever such auxiliary functions appeared to be required. It seems highly desirable that the Navy, too, possess its own fleet air arm.

The matter of being self-contained applies, however, with equal logic to the Air Force. In Britain, the R.A.F. Bomber and Fighter Commands are entirely distinct and independent of Army control. The R.A.F. Coastal Command, on the other hand, is a magnificent example of successful co-operation with another service. The Navy directs the general strategy of sea patrol, which is the special function of Coastal Command, but within this framework the Command itself is left to direct the details of actual operations.[1]

The Coastal Command has its own "marine section," and possesses a number of sea bases. It has its own shipyards complete with repair depots and workshops. There are swift boats used for rescue work, stationed at various points around the coast. There are trawlers and sixty-foot pinnaces and many other types of vessels, mostly small.

Even the R.A.F. Balloon Command is fundamentally self-contained. It has its own organization and commander-in-chief, its meteorological department,

[1] This harmonious working is insured by the provision of combined Naval and R.A.F. staffs for the Command and all Group Headquarters.

its own motor transport, medical officers, accountants, special police, and its own replacement and repair department—a depot which obviously runs to considerable proportions.

The present trend is toward the creation of the "fighter team," a co-operation phase in which the air units take a prominent place. Brilliant airmen are in control of vital sectors, such as Lieutenant General Emmons in Hawaii, and Major General Frank Andrews in the Panama Canal Zone. The War and Navy Departments now enthusiastically recognize the airplane as one of the principal instruments of combat —so much so that an old-line engineering officer recently made the amusing comment: "It looks to me like what we want now is a separate army."

Unfortunately, however, air units are considered by these Departments only in relation to their own respective spheres of activity, and in no sense as a self-reliant body with its own strategy, freedom of action and totally separate function. They can hardly be expected to conceive of air power as being capable of carrying out independent missions which under given circumstances would make their own particular Service an actual subordinate.

American air power has been seriously circumscribed as the result of being thus tied down to the ground strategy. Fighter range is limited, and until recently long-range bombers were seriously deficient both in bomb-load and firepower. This situation was the result of a dependence by ground officers on draftsmen and theoreticians for the construction of their aerial arm. Wherever the building of aircraft is dominated by the designing board alone, it will represent nothing radical or revolutionary in either bomb-load, firepower or maneuverability. The bombers, in particular, will be not much more than rebuilt airliners.

The four types of planes considered most useful to the surface forces, and in the light of whose usefulness the mission of air power was conceived, were the reconnaissance planes, built for observing, mapping and photography; the command planes which carried staff officers from one sector to another and gave a quick bird's-eye view of all operations; the dive-bomber or *Stuka* which is nothing more or less than a piece of light artillery on wings; and the hedgehopper or low-flying, ground-strafing bomber.

No sane man today can doubt the vital function of the airplane as a catalyst in any surface encounter, nor the inestimable value of the combat team of which it is a part. But to build an army dominated by a strategy alien to our geographical position, and by tactics whose peak efficiency, reached in the battles of Poland and France, is rapidly waning, is to build an army completely independent of the conditions under which it is expected to operate. The introduction of such a novelty as the combat team is by no means conclusive and represents merely an incident in military history. A comparable innovation was a dominating factor in the Battle of Hastings where an earlier fighter team, the mounted Norman knights and their accompanying archers, recast the destiny of European civilization by overwhelming the more numerous Saxon light infantry, and conquering England.

We are planning to build a stupendous 2,000,000 man air force, the world's largest, and to turn out 185,000 airplanes by the end of 1944. The substance represented by these dazzling figures would not necessarily constitute Air Power in the complete sense under discussion here, but an Army and Navy co-operation force, useful enough in its place but materially different in concept, springing from different needs, and responding to a different strategy.

The recent Army reorganization is a fine example of streamlined co-ordination between air and ground staffs, with an enormous amount of emphasis placed on the Air Forces, a recognition which could hardly be more complete. To say that the High Command thereby recognizes the importance of air power is to say that it recognizes the existence of the pyramids, or the fact that the sun rises in the east in the morning. It is utterly impossible not to recognize the importance of the air phase in any land operation. But the airplane continues to remain subordinate to Army needs and is tied close to surface tactics.[2] There is no provision for a primary air strategy, one capable of operating completely on its own as a competent and self-sufficient instrument of decision.

The new organization may be looked on as a long step forward toward the co-ordination of all armed forces under one command, with the Air Forces occupying a status equal to Army and Navy. Under the

[2] The basis for the entire setup is the creation of "cohesive fighting teams in combat under theater commanders."

present plan the commanding general of the Army
Air Forces occupies exactly the same relationship to
the Chief of Staff and the Secretary of War as does
the Commanding General of Services and Supply, and
the Commanding General of the Army Ground
Forces. Their combined relationship to all future tasks,
to strategy, to procurement and development, is a
matter of mutual integration within the office of the
Chief of Staff. It is, therefore, strictly limited. It cannot organize for a conclusive action and it cannot
even compete at the sources of political and economic
power with the other armed forces, so as to make its
demands heard. It simply takes its share and co-ordinates itself as a recognized partner in the air-land forces
working together as a team. Like the *Luftwaffe*, its
training, equipment, and activities must all be heavily
influenced by Army outlook.

Aviation has come of age and it is both dangerous
and useless to keep it tied to its mother's apron
strings. It is now by far the most powerful and potent
of all the services, and the only one available to our
use as a striking arm in the great bloody battle for
existence in which we are engaged.

Every hour in which its capacity for independent
development and action is compromised is a tragic
hour wasted.

II

"If a commander," warns Napoleon, "seeks wisdom
in debate and conferences, he must expect the result
which in all ages has followed such course; he will end
in coming to the worst possible decision, which, al-

ways in war, is the most pusillanimous, or, if you wish, the most prudent. True wisdom lies in absolute command and energetic decision."

We have come a long way down the road of military competence, but we have not as yet learned that wars cannot be won by committees, by conferences, and by debatable areas of jurisdiction. They cannot be won by seating great flyers and technicians at War Department desks to pursue purely routine administrative work. They cannot be won by politicians directing the course of military affairs, not even by the greatest and most inspired. They cannot be won by the aged, the stagnant and the decrepit, nor by too rigid an adherence to the usages of precedent.

They can only be won by unity of action, by youth, by integrity of knowledge, and by methods in which imagination and technological skill play a part. It is the unusual and the extravagant which win wars, not the stolid and the commonplace.

At this moment we are in much of the same situation as was the North during the early days of the American Civil War, when politicians drove out in carriages to watch the Battle of Bull Run from the nearby hills. It was only when President Lincoln gave tough, dour Ulysses S. Grant complete and undivided authority over the conduct of the war that the North began to win battles.

The late President Wilson was alleged to have given Black Jack Pershing a private code known only to the two of them, so that messages could go to him direct. Pershing's authority in the field was complete.

Wilson never interfered with him. The only two times the great Democrat acted contrary to the advice of General Peyton March, his Chief of Staff, was in the sending of expeditions to Siberia and Archangel. Both of these adventures, he acknowledged later, were mistakes.

Mitchell, Douhet, and de Gaulle, the great prophets of streamlined war, believed without reservation in a complete co-ordination of all the armed forces, directed under one mind. In modern warfare, said Douhet, great military commanders "can no longer be merely army, navy or air officers—they must be capable of waging war in all fields and with all types of forces." [3] You must, claimed Mitchell, have a simple commanding officer and "a sphere of command specified into which the entire air force, the sea force and all the others together go and have their work laid out." [4]

Unity of action and planning, with the authority to command their enforcement, are the only things which are effective in war. Conferences produce nothing, and the word "co-ordination" used in reference to independent units operating loosely at the discretion of their commanders, is a mere figure of speech. Such an effort at unified action as is exemplified by the Joint

[3] Louis A. Sigaud, *Douhet and Aerial Warfare*, pp. x and xi.
[4] Hearing before a Selective Committee of Inquiry, House of Representatives, Sixty-eighth Congress.
Speaking of the situation in the Hawaiian Islands in 1925, General Mitchell remarked that there was practically no co-ordination between the commanding general of the Army and the commanding admiral of the Navy. They "would not even go to the same social functions together."

Board of the Army and Navy [5] cannot produce the absolute definitions required. The board has no real authority and attempts no complex organization involving the respective bodies its members represent.

Jurisdictional jealousies still prevent the consolidation of even the intelligence and anti-sabotage agencies under a single head. These agencies include the Secret Service (a branch of the Treasury Department), the Army and Navy Intelligence Bureaus, and the FBI (Federal Bureau of Investigation).

In various of the theaters of action energetic and self-willed officers have, against all opposition, set themselves up with a chain of unified command. One of the first things Douglas MacArthur did when he became Supreme Allied Commander in the Southwest Pacific was to create a joint Australian-American military staff with absolute powers of jurisdiction, and possessing three divisions—air, army, and navy.[6]

Thus the rather ridiculous situation exists of separation and independence at home, where all vital matters of procurement, organization and action are decided, with a complete abandonment of these principles by task forces in certain vital theaters. The great confusion and basic contradictions this involves are visible at a glance. The Supreme Commander in Hawaii, an Army Air Force general, may issue orders

[5] It is composed of the Army Chief of Staff and three members of the General Staff, together with the Navy Chief of Staff and three admirals.

[6] The land forces are under the Australian, Commander General Sir Thomas Blamey; the air forces under the American, Lieutenant General George H. Brett; and the naval forces under the American, Vice-Admiral Herbert F. Leary.

to the heads of his ground and naval forces, each of whom may be receiving contradictory instructions from their Service Chiefs in Washington or even from some inconspicuous officer in one of the bureaus through channels. Back through channels must the whole business go again, to be straightened out by negotiation and discussion, wasting precious time, and forcing an unhealthy sense of frustration and annoyance on the station commanders.

In the great sea-coast bases on the American continent, the delegation of authority as between Army and Navy, and even certain non-military agencies, is vague and conflicting. Decisions involving questions of local security often have to be referred back to Washington, routed even then not through one central authority but through the desks of the various agencies involved. The Army, Navy, and Air Forces are in continual dispute over zones of authority. The Army complains, for instance, that the Navy has set up all the existing anti-aircraft guns around its own installations on the West Coast; the Air Force is resentful because the Navy has secured jurisdiction over an area of island and sea which it claims limits its plans to protect the approaches to Panama. The competition for prerogative and authority is quite open.

At headquarters, in Washington, the centripetal force of their own activities tends unavoidably to throw all of these agencies into watertight compartments burdened with jurisdictional problems and a strong spirit of mutual exclusion. There is no strong and galvanizing hand, recognized and respected by all, with authority to shear away this overgrowth of obsolescent inheritance to get down to the dynamics which lie beneath.

The National Defense chart shows that the War Department has only liaison with, but not control over, the Selective Service System. Separate and reporting only to the President, are the Department of the Navy, the Co-ordinator of Information, and the Permanent Joint Board on Defense of the United States and Canada. Another separate institution is the Council of National Defense [7] made up of the Secretaries of War, Navy, Interior, Agriculture, Commerce, and Labor, and charged with vast powers in the co-ordination of national resources.

The Office of Emergency Management, which is for all practical purposes part of the White House, in reality outranks in importance every other Government agency, including the War and Navy Departments. In complete charge of OEM, as the President's deputy, is Mr. Roosevelt's civilian adviser, Harry Hopkins, who is also chairman of the all-powerful Munitions Assignment Board which has control of "all assignments, both in quantity and priority, whether to Great Britain and the United States or other of the United Nations, in accordance with strategic needs." The tremendous potency of this Bureau requires little explanation, and the fact of its independent existence cannot help but have a determining effect on the deliberations of all the armed forces.

Through the Office of Emergency Management also flows the office of the Chairman of the War Produc-

[7] Created by Act of Congress in 1916.

tion Board, the Office of Price Administration, the Office of Civilian Defense, of Defense Aid Reports, the Defense Communications Board, the Office of Co-ordinator of Inter-American Affairs, of Defense Health and Welfare Services, the Office of Scientific Research and Development, the Division of Defense Housing Co-ordination, the Transportation Division, and the War Labor Board. This shoal of organizations is lumped together apparently without regard for kith or kind.[8] Their relationship to the armed forces is indirect and is determined by no structural consistency, a serious flaw in design which must have its corresponding effect in impairment of function.

The framework shown here does not lend itself to swift, precise, aggressive action. It is cumbersome and needs streamlining badly.

This war cannot be won by conferences and committees any more than it can be won by the countless little AEF's we are now sending all over the world. It can only be won by some great military leader who is willing to act tough and who has absolute power and authority of direction. None of the present correlating agencies is an adequate substitute for such a singleness of leadership.

The direction of the entire war effort should be handed over to a single man who has the strength to create one single vital, inspired war machine. He should have unquestioned jurisdiction over every ele-

[8] The mere fact of Mr. Hopkins' great personal ability in no sense alters the unfortunate aspect of this organizational structure.

ment of the fighting forces and be responsible only to the President of the United States and to the Congress. He should be removable, if necessary, but his work should never be directed by outside or political influence. He should be generalissimo-in-chief, director of Army, Navy, and Air Force, of all procurement, and of the Department of Psychological Warfare.

The chain of command, starting at the top, should run through the entire structure of the American warmaking machine, so that the delegation of authority would be always unequivocal and complete. In this sense we could do well to study the working mechanics of the German armed forces. Here the officer regarded as best qualified for any particular task is placed in charge. He is allowed to build his own force and to draw on any portion of the military, naval or air establishments for the purposes of his particular mission.

It is quite possible that academically, the country runs a certain risk in thus abandoning itself to the power of the military. Nevertheless, if it does not do so it is certain to have an inefficient war machine operating at cross-purposes with itself under shackled and perhaps second-rate leaders.

By virtue of his office the President of the United States is Commander-in-Chief of all the armed forces. In practice this highly specialized and complex performance has been left in the past to the management of professional soldiers who have made the business of war a lifelong study. The assumption of direct management authority and of the function of day-to-day decision on strategic matters by the political head of this Republic would be a serious operational mistake. It creates confusion and directly impedes the sound development of the military forces, making them in effect petitioners for favor and robbing them of the qualities of self-reliance and initiative.

Under the present system the military, naval and air officers merely advise the President on war strategy. The President, or the little circle of civilians around him, then decides what is to be done. This amounts not to a delegation of authority, but to the giving of individual orders which the ranking generals and admirals must then execute. Their own recommendations may be completely ignored.

No matter how one looks at the situation, from the view of ultimate values it is unsound. Much actually depends on the disposition of the President's civilian advisers, whose delegated authority is as real as if it came from him direct. If they conceive of themselves as being brilliant strategists, the military command is tied hand and foot without even the capacity for protest, while it must take the responsibility for actions dictated by non-military minds for perhaps non-military ends. This cannot help but harm the morale of the top officers, from there permeating through all ranks.

It must be pointed out in this respect, that the War Department itself, though largely regulated by military officers, is essentially a civilian agency, with a civilian representative in the President's cabinet. The right to exercise military command on the part of a civil officer subordinate to the President is a mistake and has a harmful and enervating effect on our war mechanism.[9]

Those presidents of the United States who have operated successfully in crises have not attempted to interfere with the handling of military campaigns. Said General Grant of Lincoln: "All he wanted or had ever wanted was someone who would take the responsibility and act, and call on him for all the assistance needed, pledging himself to use all the power of the Government in rendering such assistance." [10] Of Wilson, Herring remarks: "The President had the sound administrative sense to delegate responsibility and leave his subordinates free to carry their full burden of authority within their respective fields." [11]

Questions of tactics and strategy, as well as technical problems relating to other details of operation, should be decided by others qualified for these purposes, though the chain of authority should begin with the Chief Executive and flow through his office. "There can be no more dangerous bottleneck than congestion of power at the top." [12]

The President of the United States occupies an exalted position which removes him completely from the personal handling of all administrative tasks. He is the balance wheel, the absolute and final authority which co-ordinates the political, the economic, and

[9] An excellent discussion on this point is contained in Pendleton Herring's book, *The Impact of War*, pp. 150-165.

[10] *Personal Memoirs of Ulysses S. Grant*, Vol. II, p. 122; cf. Pendleton Herring, *The Impact of War*, p. 154.

[11] Pendleton Herring, *The Impact of War*, p. 155.

[12] Ibid., p. 160.

the military into one mighty unit. His fingers must be on the pulse of the American people at all times. He is the judge, the conciliator, and vicar of our Republic, to whom all branches of the government, legislative, executive and judicial, must look for leadership. The Departments of the Treasury, of State, of Labor, and Agriculture come under his jurisdiction as well as the War and Navy Departments. The Office of Emergency Management, the Board of Economic Warfare, and all the other factors and forces which flow into the office of the Chief Executive of the United States are his business and require his attention. His is the office where all the conflicting and varied forces which go to make up a great self-governing state meet to co-ordinate themselves in one mighty river of activity. With all due respect to his person, it is not given to the President of the United States, although he is actually the Commander-in-Chief, to direct the details of strategy and organization of the armed services.

As yet no such thing exists as a compact, hard-driving, synchronized leadership for the so-called United Nations. The whole question of unity is still in the academic stage.

Russia keeps itself aloof. China is willing but inaccessible. Holland, Poland, Norway and the others are not much more than names on the morning roll-call. Canada does not even have conscription for fear of offending her intransigeant French population.

Britain and Australia, like *Barkus*, seem to be willing to make a try at the business, but not much has as yet come of it. In Washington there now sits a combined Chiefs of Staff group composed of American and British Army, Navy, and Air officers. Its powers are limited to those of discussion and recommendation. If the Joint Anglo-American Staff is to have power and usefulness and be anything else than a high-flown debating society, it must possesss a directing head capable of making any decision he deems necessary relative to the conduct of this war; and it must be invested with absolute powers to determine strategy and to act in the name of the governments involved.

If this agency were set up seriously, with the required authority, it could become the nucleus for a great war-making apparatus involving all of the twenty-eight United Nations. It should be constituted as a super-staff with authority to tap all resources of manpower, industry or wealth of the nations concerned, with only one end in view—to win the war. It should be the starting point of a whole chain of authority which reaches down into every aspect of our own national effort, as well as into the war effort of our allies.

Economic unity for the purposes of prosecuting the conflict should be established as an integral part of this operation. This super-staff would decide who makes what, where it is to be shipped, and how. It would determine the plans for utilizing such bottoms as we may possess between us, or which may be later acquired. All of this would feed directly into the military office, and not have to involve circumlocutory tracks to a number of civilian agencies or other governmental bureaus.

There should be one master blueprint for everything, for military strategy, for psychological war, for industrial construction, for tactics and planning. An auxiliary planning committee, handled by a small group of able and imaginative men, would form a special geo-physical bureau, which would view strategic action on a global scale, and attempt to both anticipate and force events. It would co-ordinate the planning staffs of all the United Nations, and its initiative of action would breathe vitality into the war-making schemes of the entire anti-Axis coalition. Compared to the gigantic Geopolitical Institute of General Karl Haushofer, which has been operating for a full generation, our proposed planning board would be largely makeshift, but it would give the war forces of the United Nations a co-ordination they now lack.

At the head of this Gargantuan combat mechanism, we could do worse than to place the giant Frenchman, de Gaulle. If clairvoyance and a close apprehension of problems to be met in future constitute military genius, de Gaulle is the greatest soldier alive, but a leader without an army. To place him in command of the United Nations' war forces would be a political master stroke, in addition to an act of military consequence. The effect it would have on the Latin nations of Europe, of Spain, Italy, and France, now told with some effect that the war has settled into an Anglo-Saxon effort to control the world, would be incalculable.

III

It must now be recognized by military scientists that the waging of modern war on a total basis involves simultaneous action on a number of different levels. This is not only a war of machines and supply lines but also a war of ideas, and when the history of our times is finally written it may be proven that the most important auxiliary to the big bomber was not the panzer division but those ghostly elements which wage war for possession of the human mind. Thus three-dimensional warfare would find its natural ally in the strange world of the fourth dimension. The fact that a new combat technique may not be measurable in terms of calipers and a slide-rule, by no means rules it out as a task force.

This unique combat column, whose ammunition is words and whose net is a skillful entanglement of ideas, goes generally under the name of psychological warfare. The question is not whether our military leaders should recognize it—but whether they dare ignore it. On the record alone, there are often times when psychological warfare is the most potent weapon in the entire arsenal of Mars, a dangerous, unseen destroyer which can affect an adversary with all the suddenness of a plague.

The tendency in our country today is to regard this essential activity as either a propaganda agent designed to promote certain idealistic theories in human relationship, or as a vehicle to voice the convictions of political and military leaders. Actually psychological warfare is neither: it is a technique of attack supplementing the other attack columns. It can be concerned only with those activities which in themselves are a distinct aid to the military and which promote the winning of the war.

The ammunition of this conflict of ideas is as impersonal as a demolition bomb. The technique may not at any point be designed along ideological lines, but only along those coldly practical and functional channels which directly fit in with the strategy of the military and meet its needs. Military propaganda is a weapon of war and, like any other task force, it should be related to a timed objective which is part of the master plan of operation. It is as much a part of tactics as the big howitzers, the aircraft carriers, or our fleets of bombers. It may not be sent on ridiculous missions without hurtful results, and to misunderstand its qualities for good or bad is to render it useless altogether. Even more truly than with the strategy of armed forces, perfect timing dictates the quality of its success.

Every military advance should be preceded and accompanied by a barrage of propaganda activity aimed not only at disrupting the enemy, and undermining his faith in his cause and the strength and honor of his leaders, but at deluding and deceiving him as to our actual military purpose, lulling him to a feeling of security and, if possible, taking the initiative away from him and placing him on the defensive. Any activity which serves these purposes, which tends to promote fear, disunity, hysteria, and disintegration, or leads to dissatisfaction and revolt, is a desirable one and should be used. The mission of psychological warfare is best explained by the Nazi oracle, Dr. Banse: "The enemy nation's originally solid, powerful and well-knit fabric," he admonishes, "must be gradually dissolved, broken down and rotted, so that it falls apart like a fungus stepped on in the forest."

With this arm alone Hitler was enabled to conquer whole countries without a blow, and has prepared others for the kill so that the military could move in on a disrupted and disorganized defense. "The Germans have staked rich claims on the use of psychology in total war," comments the monograph *German Psychological Warfare*. And says Edmond Taylor: "Never has the world seen propaganda in all its forms used on such a tremendous scale, with so much precision and efficacy as in this war of nerves which is really an invisible war of wills." [13]

The Germans have spent fabulous sums on propaganda organization and have created an awesome maze of organizations whose target is not the bodies of other men, but their minds, souls, and social structures. The net is cast wide. Every possible resource which can contribute to the waging of this strange form of war is explored, tested, and organized. The countries which are to be attacked are studied thoroughly and innumerable analyses made of their national character, their social and political conditions, the economic strains and racial differences which exist, as well as every other possible avenue of difference and inequality which may be exploited.

The wiles of professional diplomacy are not an ade-

[13] *The Strategy of Terror*, p. 69.

quate substitute for this form of offensive action. They will be brushed aside by the onrush of events as if they were so many cobwebs. Only a deliberate attempt, rolling against the bastions of the opposition in unceasing waves and implemented with every element of the psychologist's and propagandist's skill, can serve a useful purpose. The structure of the Nazi party, its antagonisms, divergencies, and contradictions should be minutely studied. The economic system of Germany, its inequalities and its failures, should be examined with a jeweler's glass, and heavy wedges should be driven in all the cracks which show themselves.

All good observers who have been in the Reich mention the fact that the German suffers from an inferiority complex which is part of the whole system of grossness and vulgarity which allows him to reach forward to the state of *uebermensch*. The German, says Wallace Deuel, "is essentially unsure of himself. He lacks poise. More, he is chaotic and violent. He is a creature of constant 'Sturm and Drang,' of storm and strength and striving, of self-consciousness and self-examination." [14]

Within Germany itself there still remains a considerable amount of sabotage and fifth-column effort, of resistance to the regime. Machines are damaged and trains derailed. Illegal newspapers are still very much alive, as is the illegal radio which moves from place to place. The Nazis repress all information about this phenomenon, but it nevertheless exists.

The industrialists of Germany, as well as the mid-

[14] *People Under Hitler*, pp. 24-25.

dle-class business men, are now in the hands of Nazi Party bureaucrats and are ruled by commissars. These people, whose purblind greed helped to bring on the Fascist wave of terror, have lost no part of the miserable qualities they possessed before. Vindictive hatred must have added to them. There is also a constant conflict between the army and the Gestapo which can be exploited, as well as the struggle between the Nazi Party radicals and the Reichswehr officer caste.

The German authorities have through every means impressed on the German people that they belong to a superior race, that they are utterly invincible. German internal propaganda shows all opponents to be sub-human creatures who can never be expected to resist the iron-handed, sharp-bladed German soldier. The reality will come as a tremendous shock to the German people when literal hell is bombed out of them. The contrast between fact and fiction is a psychological maze in which the German morale must lose its way and collapse. Our entire propaganda should be aimed at terrifying, intimidating, confusing, and disrupting the Germans. Every aerial attack should be accompanied by leaflets and preceded and followed by the blasts of radio voices, reminding the Germans of their crimes and holding out the absolute certainty of punishment.

The Nazi structure is honeycombed throughout with graft; the whole system of power and ruthlessness in itself breeds not faith but mutual distrust. It is perfectly well known in Germany that a sufficient sum will buy anything from passport papers to escape from prison. The whirl of corruption which the Nazi hierarchy swills in, the pagan opportunism which dominates their philosophy, will finally wreck them. Bribery, direct and indirect, state-sanctioned looting, ordinary petty thievery, assault and murder, have taken a fearful toll of Nazi character. These are the supermen of the new Europe, a gang of cruel and unscrupulous plunderers, whose mischievous instincts can be turned inward into mutual suspicion, fear, and hatred.

It should be easy to destroy the faith of the German mass in the omniscience of its leaders. The continuous Hitler assurances of "final victory" to come next month or next year are ample evidence of the apprehension held by the German rulers on the morale front. There are reports of hysteria, of tremendous public weariness, and of enormous fear among the German population. German morale is fundamentally unsound. The only thing which holds the Reich together today is the expectation of final victory. When the Germans have been caused to believe that their expectation of triumph is a vain one the beginning of the end will be in sight. Our offensive must match the certainty of terrible defeat, phrase for phrase and word for word, with the effort of the German propaganda machine to create the impression of ultimate victory. The over-use of such words as democracy and freedom will produce no result whatsoever. The German people have no feeling for democracy and, at best, consider it a debatable topic.

In conjunction with our air and sea attacks on Nippon also, we can use psychological warfare with deadly effect. The inconsistencies of Japanese national life, the incongruities which exist between its modern industrial economy and the feudal system which controls its social and political life, can be exploited to the hilt and timed so that the maximum weight of the blow falls exactly during the period of our greatest military offensive. Japan is full of contradictions of the most abrasive nature. Chamberlin speaks of "the characteristic feelings of the Japanese military fanatics; hatred of the wealthy classes of financiers and bureaucrats, the strain of Puritanism and exalted conception of the position of the emperor, and of Japan's world mission." [15] Despite the existence of the fantastically wealthy houses of Mitsui and Mitsubishi which would appear to make Japan a stronghold for reactionary individualism, the army itself, and especially the younger officers, is highly socialistic. The Press Bureau of the War Department issued a pamphlet in 1934 calling for an abandonment of the present capitalist system of free competition and the establishment of a collectivist economy. This would mean the complete destruction of the money barons and the great industrial houses. Manchukuo, itself, is now ruled by the army with an iron hand as a collectivist experiment. Just as the army is largely of peasant origin, the navy draws its numbers largely from the nobility and upper classes, and a great feeling of tension and competition exists between the two bodies.

Nor may the so-called rice riots of August 1918, in which several million Japs were involved, be forgotten. It was necessary to call in the army, as well as the po-

[15] William Henry Chamberlin, *Japan Over Asia*, p. 257.

lice, to suppress them. The result was the resignation of an entire Japanese cabinet. In 1931 there were 2456 labor disputes in Japan. There has been a consistent growth of labor and tenant farmer unions and other forms of resistance to the rise of military Fascism. As late as 1937, more than 3000 anti-Fascists were arrested within a period of two months in the great industrial and commercial centers. In this year strikes increased to 6170, many of them in armament factories. Despite the feudal circumstances under which Japan is governed, the veneration of the emperor's household and the enormous patriotism which verges on the fanatic, Japan is far from impregnable to a war of ideas. By an ably handled effort it can be put on the defensive and gradually disintegrated from within.

It should not be forgotten that 5,000,000 Chinese live and grumble on strategic Formosa. They have practically no place in the government or civil service and receive far less pay than that accorded Japanese workmen doing identical types of labor. Here is the nucleus for a powerful fifth column. Korea, too, still retains its historical enmity for the conqueror.

In Manchukuo the rule of the Japanese bureaucrat and soldier has resulted in many irritations. Natives are permitted for the most part to execute only unskilled labor. The engineers, professional men, business men, and executives, together with the white collar workers, are almost entirely Japanese. Chamberlin states that the South Manchuria Railway did not report a single Chinese among its 180 higher officials and its 134 engineers in 1934, and that there are only seventy-one Chinese among its 5608 clerical workers.

It is perfectly believable that resentment and frustration must boil high among the native Manchurians whose education and training would qualify them for political or economic posts. This area is ripe for insurrection. Japanese soldiers are assassinated regularly. The part that well-handled instigation can play is indicated in the sudden defection of the Mongol General Pai Feng-hsiang's army of 18,000 cavalrymen, together with their Japanese-supplied equipment, as a result of a minor quarrel during the spring of 1942. These Mongols have now joined forces with the Chinese.

The Japanese cannot avoid knowing what the result must be when the two great Axis partners face each other across the boundaries of Central Asia, with all the rest of the world devoured. Their conflicting ambitions and the factors which predispose toward them, can be played on now, and the natural suspicion with which they regard each other can be exploited for all it is worth. Germany still considers itself as the rightful possessor of the Netherlands colonies of the East Indies and has never acknowledged their possession by Japan. The Reich simply looks on this as a temporary concession to the realities.

We cannot begin too early in an effort aimed at splitting Germany from her allies. The various nations in the Axis are known to fear and detest each other. The disorganization, the disillusionment, and the unhappiness of Fascist Italy, of Hungary, Rumania, and the other satellites of the German Reich, should all be patiently and systematically nurtured. Every vexatious plan and scheme which might be fitted into the breach of the propaganda gun should be used. No one will be able to take away from us the initiative which such an offensive automatically creates. We will be striking at the enemy with this weapon day and night with increasing skill, shrewdness, and wisdom, creating opportunities for the other task forces and easing their path of conquest.

All reports indicate that Italian soldiers hate the Nazis bitterly and the Nazis, in turn, are said to be utterly contemptuous of the Italians. In Lybia this has resulted in endless brawls. The Appenine Peninsula, itself, is said to be rife with anti-Fascist sentiment. A bloodless revolution deposing Mussolini would be certain except for the fear of Hitler's legions sitting on the Brenner Pass, which would come smashing down to take control in name as well as in reality. The Italian people have something of an idea of how Hitler treats subject races who are not favored by him. Italy is run for Hitler by the *Italian Korps*, Germans who wear Italian uniforms and operate in key spots. The Gestapo has Italy well in hand. Here again is a weak point in the Axis structure which a well-calculated assault in the psychological sphere might be able to crack.

All Europe is a hotbed in which fear and animal weariness vie with hatred and the desire for violence. In every country German emigrés have come in the van of the marching armies and have taken over the banks, the businesses, and all lucrative posts. Loot of every description pours out of these impoverished places and into the cities of the Reich. At the very first hint of German defeat, says Harsch, "the subject populations would rise in a fury and not one of these Germans who are living off their backs, would remain alive. The Germans are perfectly aware of this." [16] These interlopers are detested even more than the iron fist of the German army or the calculated fury of the Gestapo.

The whole Continent is ripe for propaganda direction that can be told by radio, by word of mouth, and any one of the numerous ways which the complex art of psychological warfare has developed. Sabotage, insurrection, and assassination are today merely spontaneous actions on the part of individuals, of small groups of men, or the larger guerrilla armies which operate behind the German lines in Serbia, Poland, Russia, and Greece. None of these men have any cohesive direction. Certainly their cohorts in the cities and farmsteads are given no intelligent, tangible leadership. To a certain degree this is tried from Britain under the auspices of an announcer who is simply called Colonel Britton, but as an organized, carefully thought-out plan, audacious in its technique and clever in its strategy, it leaves much to be desired.

It is assumed that our military authorities are in active touch with such major guerrilla detachments as that of General Draja Mikhailovitch who operates out of mountain headquarters in Jugoslavia with what is said to be over 100,000 fighters. There are large bands in Manchuria and Korea, in Greece, and other places; but there are also the far vaster bodies of the unorganized who are waiting patiently for the day of vengeance. In Czechoslovakia, where no major guerrilla

[16] *Pattern of Conquest*, pp. 46-47.

warfare goes forward, groups of patriots cut telephone lines, derail troop and ammunition trains, or blow up armament factories. At the Skoda works 113 men were executed at a single stroke by the Gestapo for sabotage. In Holland 500 Dutchmen were arrested in one day in reprisal for bombings.[17] In Norway terror and counter-terror have become a daily feature of life. In Greece, contaminated by the unrest around them, several Austrian units are stated to have revolted against German military officers and killed a number of them. In Belgium so many people have been arrested that at St. Gillis prison, on the outskirts of Brussels, five or six prisoners occupy a cell intended for one. According to the Swedish paper, *Ny Dag*, 125 trains have been derailed in three months, and telephone and telegraph wires have been cut 405 times. The largest single stroke of sabotage occurred in Norway, where over 100 German transports and supply ships were blown up by Norwegian patriots all in the same hour, just before dawn on January 10, 1942.

It is possible to lead and direct this huge spontaneous movement which rises out of the instincts and hatreds of the dispossessed. Agents may be landed among these people by parachute, and they will be harbored and protected. The local populations can be organized into tremendous mass espionage societies if the United Nations so will it. The positions of ships, the dispositions of troops, the locations of plants, air fields and gun emplacements, the organization of sabotage and even of *franc-tireur* bands, come well within the possible scope of activity.

[17] March 1, 1942.

It would be useful to tell the suffering victims to keep a record of the crimes committed against them by their conquerors, so that the criminals will be made to pay individually as well as collectively, when the day comes.[18] This could easily be part of the war of nerves against the invader, and may already have played an important part in, for instance, the assassination of Heydrich.

Whatever means we devise must at least be related to the military scheme—it cannot be concerned with mere garrulous platitudes. It must be concerned with the actual realities as they exist today. What, for example, must be the reaction of a tortured German anti-Nazi hiding out in a cellar in Berlin, or those rebellious bitter men who are putting up a last-ditch guerrilla fight in the hills and forests of Poland, Greece, and Jugoslavia, when they read a document like the Atlantic Charter? The question we must ask ourselves is simply this: Is such a document as the cor-

[18] The governments of the countries occupied by Germany met in London early in January 1942, to discuss German violations of the laws of nations and humanity and to formulate a policy in regard to them. Among the conclusions reached was that the United Nations "place among their principal war aims the punishment through the channel of organized justice of those guilty and responsible for these crimes whether they have ordered them, perpetrated them, or in any way participated in them . . . (and) see to it that (a) those guilty and responsible . . . are sought for, handed over to justice and judged; (b) that the sentences pronounced are carried out. The position is quite clear in reference to the necessity for the summary punishment of those who made the war, who encouraged its terrorist methods in the occupied countries, as well as those who committed the actual crimes, and of the Quislings who aided and abetted the aggressors." The signatory representatives attending were from the governments of Belgium, Czechoslovakia, Free French National Committee, Greece, Luxembourg, Netherlands, Norway, Poland, and Jugoslavia.

nerstone of our effort, a stimulant to the will to resist on the part of our smashed allies? Can a man who has been tortured, whose home has been burned over his head, whose women have been degraded, and who has passed through the hell of German sadism and cruelty, be ennobled by the promise to secure for the German aggressor guarantees against territorial changes and "access on equal terms to the trade and to the raw materials of the world which are needed for their economic prosperity" after the war is over?

What these ruined people want is hard, bitter talk related exactly to their own problems. They want to be told exactly what to do—just the opposite of what we are telling them. "They do not want general exhortations on the subject of democracy. That makes them ill. They want direction as to how they can save themselves and rebuild their world. They want specific facts as to what we are doing about it." [19]

These exhortations to democracy and morality are very nice, but they do not fit in with the major problem which is that of winning a war. What possible effect can the Atlantic Charter have on the Nazi German himself? Is he not told to be calm, and is he not given every assurance which good morale demands? The situation to him is clear. If Hitler wins, he will be a member of the privileged class, the class of *uebermenschen*, who will rule the globe completely, who will make physical slaves of all other peoples including the Americans, and who alone will have the right to possess property, maintain industry, armed forces, or educational institutions. And if this vigorous thrust

[19] Arthur Upham Pope in *Free World*, March 1942.

for world domination should fail, even then Hitler would be proven right, for the Germans will still have more than they were able to obtain under the democratic Reich, since they have not only been promised independence and territorial integrity, *but complete and equal access to all the world's raw materials.*

This is a strange reward for international criminality and banditry. Whatever folly of appeasement the traditional sentimentality of the great English-speaking nations may lead us into after the war, it is psychologically unsound to offer it now.

The writer has talked to many well-informed Europeans and there are none who venture to suggest that sugary promises or soft handling will have the slightest effect upon the German nation. If ever a war was a total expression of the will and psychology of an entire people, this one is of German lawlessness and will to power. No political leader in modern times has had the support, verging on religious adoration, which has been given Adolf Hitler. Whoever misunderstands the blind fanaticism of the German nation, its cruelty, sadism, and hatred for the democratic way of life, its megalomaniac belief in the power of force and the right of German blood to rule and to relegate all others to the position of a sub-human species, utterly misunderstands the quality and causes of this war.[20]

To break up German morale at home it is necessary to visit ruin and destruction on their houses and

[20] Declared President Benes of Czechoslovakia: "Unless we make it clear that aggressive war will always involve punishment of the nation which provoked it, and that civilized men simply will not accept any crude racial theories, or other Nazi theories about the 'Herren-volk,' I can see no hope for Europe or humanity."

industries so that it is visible to all eyes. Instead of appealing to a non-existent or suppressed generosity, kindness, and idealism, it is necessary to work on German fears, on their mutual hatreds and jealousies. They should be treated as pariahs, as beyond the realm of decent human society, and threatened with absolute and inevitable punishment for their crimes. So, too, should the Quislings and traitors in the various countries, who should not be led to believe complacently that they will escape retribution. We, in short, must take the offensive psychologically, leaving appeasement and defense far behind. Then when the Germans are bombed out of house and factory, fear and terror will strike the fainthearted, a contaminating disease when once introduced. The corruption of panic will begin to make itself felt; they will quarrel among themselves and mistrust their leaders' judgment. All that is craven and cowardly in their make-up will bubble to the surface. Each inexorable blow at their cities by our winged avengers will hasten the process of disintegration.

We should adopt a reasoned attitude toward every part of this program based on computations whose only end purpose is to see the Axis beaten and disillusioned so that resistance comes to an end as quickly as possible. The weapon of psychological attack, the same as any other, should be viewed only with an eye to its destructive power, to its ability to shatter the enemy at every front at which you can get at him. If it is unethical to smash him by every trick of expressed hatred and propaganda, then it is equally immoral for us to build instruments of death with which to splatter his blood all over the continents of Mother Earth until he submits and yields his infamous design of conquest.

The first rule of war is to destroy the enemy—not give him hope—and any instrument which assists in that design is useful. It we do not take an aggressive, shrewd, cold stand on this question we will find ourselves in full retreat on the psychological front because the Germans and the Japanese have long since built their positions for an attack in force on exactly this line. Possession of the initiative in the psychological sphere almost gave Hitler the world. Its possession is a precious military asset in a universe in which the military, the political, and the economic have merged into one.

In our country and, indeed, in the United Nations generally, with the exception of a few half-hearted efforts which have neither continuity nor power, no real attempt is made along this line. In America there is a small unit tucked away somewhere under the Joint Chiefs of Staff which goes under the title of the Joint Psychological Warfare Branch, but it has very little real power. The Office of the Co-ordinator of Information, which controls all radio broadcasts to Europe and Asia, has been merged with the new Office of War Information, whose function will apparently be largely internal and informative. A great portion of the personnel of the COI has been assigned by a separate military order to the United States Joint Chiefs of Staff to act as a special information service for the General Staff under the name of Office of Strategic Services. The Office of the Co-ordinator of Latin-

American Affairs continues to remain independent, apparently without any direct relationship to the plans of the military forces.[21]

All of these minor efforts could easily be discarded in favor of a gigantic Bureau of Psychological Warfare, directly associated with the planned air offensive. American psychologists, sociologists, and other thinkers have led the world. If these men were inducted into the American war machine and their studies carefully indexed, sifted, and tested in the field, the same as any other war-time operation, it would have a tremendous effect in shortening the period of the war and in guaranteeing that victory we seek. These men, the scientists and the thinkers, queer and obtuse as they may appear to be to orthodox military eyes, possess the crystal-clear mind and the omniscient insight into human character and behavior which would enable us to wage war in the fourth dimension against the Germans and Japanese, as well as in the first, second, and third. And they do not require any involved apparatus. All they need is protection, quiet, a room with a table and some chairs, pencils, and some paper.

IV

As we have seen, the keynote to modern war is elasticity, imagination, and alertness. Methods which are successful in one situation fail dismally in another.

[21] The Germans meanwhile have been particularly clever in exploiting the Spanish *Falange* to build up hatred against the United States in Latin America, and as a long-range adjunct to their military scheme.

The army and tactics which would serve Britain separated by twenty-two miles of water from the continent of Europe, would be the prelude to an overnight collapse if applied to Russia.

A hidebound general staff, wedded to the past, is an incompetent general staff. It is a dangerous state of mind which scoffs at the capacity of an original and revolutionary mind like Hitler's to create strategy and lead tactics and which at the same time will reward some dull intelligence like Gamelin's with the reverence accorded genius. As far as capacity is concerned, the exact opposite may be and often is true, as when an inspired dialectician like Trotsky, unencumbered by any great amount of classic military knowledge, succeeds in leading a rabble to victory over the best-trained tacticians in Europe.

De Gaulle points out that since the army lives by stability, conformity, and tradition, it "instinctively fears anything that tends to modify its structure." [22] "We know that all professions develop rigidities," comments Pendleton Herring.[23] And says Alexander Severus: "There is hardly an aspect of military life which does not display an amazing collection of carefully preserved antiquities." [24]

Just as the American General Staff considered Mitchell extreme, and the French thought de Gaulle's ideas fantastic, so, long before, the cross-bow was looked on contemptuously as an effeminate arm by

[22] *The Army of the Future*, p. 176.
[23] *The Impact of War*, p. 53.
[24] "The Fetish of Military Rank," *Military Affairs*, Journal of the American Military Institute, Fall 1941 issue.

the brawny welders of the long-bow it was to sup-
plant. In every age and at every period resistance to
innovation has been the military habit. Only when
the new weapon could no longer be refused was it
widely adopted. It was the German artillery arm itself
which was the center of the opposition to Count von
Schlieffen's efforts to create a mobile heavy artillery,
as it was the Junker army caste which fought the inno-
vations demanded by the Nazi firebrands.

During peace time in a democratic society the armed
forces tended to become a forgotten and isolated
group. They were regarded by our Republic and its
political leaders as pretty much a liability, to be
tolerated but not encouraged. To obtain the most
urgently required appropriations the military leadership was forced to lobby on the social-political fringe
and to bring every possible influence to bear.

The whole system leaned toward a stratification of
values and a lowering of aggressive vigor. Promotion
was usually the result not of great capacity, unusual
daring, imagination and shrewdness, but of an ability
to save pennies, to cut corners—that is, of fine administrative capacities—abilities which are not necessarily applicable to military leadership in time of war.

The most brilliant men were employed on the inevitable staff work, and loaded down with bureaucratic routine. Problems were reduced to long-winded
files which made the rounds of all the departments
which bore any relation to them. These sometimes
acquired the proportions of telephone books and in
them inspiration and initiative died.

The result was to place a premium on regularity

and conservatism. The surest guide to promotion was regularity and an adherence to the social graces, while political connections, too, could be helpful.

Boldness and original thinking usually brought an officer into headlong collision with his seniors and did not pay off. The whole business was bound up with the invidious "files," a criterion which was never more ridiculous and dangerous than it is at this moment of World War and international crisis. The less a man does, the fewer antagonisms he raises among his fellow officers, the more he is willing to compromise and buttress his decisions with the approval of his superiors, the more certain it is that his record will entitle him to promotion.

There is also an unfortunate tendency toward stratifying officers in certain positions for which they seem to be peculiarly qualified. For instance, a man of great capacity might be found to fill a certain obscure staff job well and is afterward regarded as "irreplaceable." This in itself, no matter how capable he might be, is practically sufficient to bar him from promotion.

When danger threatens the country, the somnambulant peace-time routine is suddenly interrupted and the Republic expects a miracle in shrewdness and enterprise from the same military bodies it had condemned for a generation to the most sterile routine. Such an overnight transformation is obviously an impossibility. The armed forces suddenly taken out of the moth balls in which they have lain all these years, simply cannot measure up to these extraordinary expectations. They require time to throw off their own dead-wood, to recover from the terrific shock of sudden and unprecedented expansion, and to adjust themselves to a whole new set of conditions for which they are ill prepared.

Under the circumstances it is phenomenal that we have been able to accomplish what we have accomplished. When the rule of relativity is applied, our success has been fantastic. But we have a long way yet to go.

The old bureaucratic peace-time routine still hamstrings the Army's efforts. Subordinates are afraid to risk making decisions. Matters which could be expeditiously settled by a simple discussion between men at neighboring desks, must make the circle as memoranda and have as many as eight, ten or more signatures affixed to them, by which time they often die of inertia.

The situation drastically requires reform. In the present situation a subordinate in one of the bureaus, who gets his rank, say, from the Air Corps, may be promoted to a full colonel, whereas the chief of the department may be only a lieutenant colonel or a major. Leading figures in the War Department, on whom we should rely for decision and boldness of concept, are so overloaded with inter-departmental administrative details that they have practically no time to give to the larger problems of war and strategy. Officers may not hire or fire their stenographic help or other office workers, even for the most flagrant inefficiency.

In the Officer Candidates Schools the antiquated

technique includes such routine as punching dummies through the middle in bayonet practice and policing the grounds for cigarette stubs and old papers. The qualifications demanded for officer training bear little relation to practical considerations. In the air branch those not blessed with a classical education have little chance. Yet Eddie Rickenbacker, one of the greatest of our pilots, never got out of public school. Another American, Homer Barry, who became a great English pilot, never went to any school. In England and Germany, if an applicant can count and read, or otherwise show qualities of initiative and leadership, he will be allowed to carry on. In this country, of every hundred flying cadet applicants only twenty are able to pass the rigid physical and mental tests. About half of those rejected had only minor deficiencies.

The one impressive thing about the Axis armies is the high degree of practical co-ordination which distinguishes them; the sense of realism with which they approach their problems—and, strangely enough, the absolute democratization of the leadership selection process. Out of the whole welter of Nazi corruption the one institution which is kept absolutely clean is the Army. There is but one criterion for promotion and that is ability. Neither birth nor connections, nor any other relationship helps—not even Party connections. Harsch informs us that an army maneuver in Germany is not just an abstract exercise but a ruthlessly employed means of finding ability and rejecting incompetence. The officer who handles his troops well and wins a tactical success in maneuvers, is instantly advanced. Officers who fail in the field are demoted, actually down to the ranks if their deficiencies are glaring enough.[25]

The Germans operate their system for selecting officer material according to the most modern methods. From the instant a recruit enters the armed forces he is subject to aptitude tests and an endless number of analyses in which every conceivable scientific personality test is used.

The Germans employ a great number of scientists on this work, as well as regular *Reichswehr* officers. Candidates for officers' posts are appraised for technical skill, mental energy, clear thinking and readiness to carry plans through to the limit of physical endurance. "Formal knowledge is explicitly stated as being of secondary importance to the spiritual qualities and emotional attitudes of the soldier." [26] An elaborate technique is used to select officers and specialists. This includes the study of the applicant's life history, his facial expressions, appearance, voice, and speech. These are carefully analyzed in detail according to methods which have been developed in the psychological laboratories. Even handwriting analysis is given serious attention. Intelligence and interest tests are used, while alertness, manual dexterity and the ability to express himself logically, are also measured, together with memory and speed of physical or motor response. "The tests require two full days in the army

[25] Joseph C. Harsch, *Pattern of Conquest.*
[26] *German Psychological Warfare*, p. 18.

and two and a half in the air force, during which the candidates are confined to the testing station." [27]

The qualities looked for in officers are imagination, ability to learn quickly, initiative, and the capacity for leadership. There is no rote memory examination except for future liaison officers, who are required to repeat complicated reports of the kind they will use later in actual training and combat.

There is also included a general appraisal of ability and native intelligence, which is weighed independent of the total of the tests. A full record is kept of the officer's work in the field, his competence in directing men, his capacity to meet situations, his resourcefulness, and his efficiency under difficult conditions.

Special stress is laid on new ideas and each year the War Ministry gives all officers the opportunity to write prize theses on military subjects. Visionary schemes which bear relation to the proposed plan of action are all entertained, such as the landing of troops by gliders, or a technique for invasion of a difficult mountain country. A bright young man may start from nowhere and become a general in his early forties.

Men who display first-class qualities of leadership are patiently developed and sent through all the important branches of the field forces. They spend a period in the Air Corps where they are taught to fly everything from a dive-bomber to the big four-engine jobs. They are made at home in every phase of aerial strategy. They operate panzer regiments and serve with the infantry and engineers. Selected groups have

[27] *German Psychological Warfare*, pp. 20-21.

also been given two years with the navy, serving on submarines, capital ships and other vessels, to learn naval tactics at first hand. These officers are now nicknamed "the three-dimensionalists" because of their general knowledge of the entire military, air and naval apparatus, giving them an ability to command equaled by few other officer groups in the world.

The results of this training were quite apparent in the conquest of Norway, in the battles of the Low Countries and of France, in the Serbian and Greek campaigns, and in the Battle of Crete, all of which ran in the face of military tradition and presented difficult problems which would have deterred almost any normal military man.

The German is taught to think in terms of the entire team or national armed force and not in terms of his own branch. The competitive factor is never allowed to turn inward and is forced out on the circumference where it belongs.

In many of its aspects the British air corps system of personnel selection is akin to that of the Germans. The elasticity and competence of its method of sifting for ability are undoubtedly responsible for much of this body's efficiency. There is no such thing as a man volunteering for officer training—that is, to become part of the gentleman's caste. The volunteer simply offers himself for air crew duties and passes through three successive stages: ground training, initial training, and service flying. In each of these he is given a psychological appraisal by a special officer, which carries equal weight with the physical and mental tests to which he is put. Rejectees, if mechanically inclined, are automatically fitted into ground crew work or shifted over to the various trades.

As with the Germans, the quality of leadership is placed foremost in judging the capacities of each student. Minor defects such as bad eyes, which may be handled by corrective goggles, do not disqualify. Putting his finger on the point, the commander of a large training center said to the author: "Whether the applicant has a classical knowledge or not does not mean a damn to us."

If a man be intelligent and able, with leadership qualifications, even though unlettered, he is taught enough mathematics to qualify as a navigator. He only needs a simple basis of algebra—enough elementary mathematics to handle simple calculations quickly and accurately. Instead of the usual arbitrary educational tests, special psychological or reaction tests are used as laid down by Professor Bartlett. The crews are also made as interchangeable as possible, a system which has great merit since if either navigator or pilot is knocked out by a stray shot, the ship still can carry on.

It is obvious that where great stresses are placed on initiative, boldness, and imagination, you get quite another sort of leadership than where plodding regularity and the rule of promotion by seniority are in effect. This rule raised out of the small, professional peace-time army a considerable group of officers who attained their rank simply because they had been in the service a certain number of years "and not at all because they had ever been drastically and competitively rated on their ability to do the job they'd have to do in war." [28]

Such an armed force, lost in the maze of many years of peace, its affairs all but liquidated by a political and economic system which looked down on the military with unconcealed disparagement, tended to inter all its thinking within the stratified layers of the General Staff. Tactics and organization followed studied precedent, submerging original thought and drowning the initiative of the commander in a vast ocean of staff work. Despite the high proportion of brilliant individual officers this condition hardly made for full efficiency.

Our officers corps has been supplemented by the granting of commissions to a considerable number of capable civilian specialists and by recalling the large group of reservists into active service. Most of these are on the elderly side and have little if any training in the methods of modern war. As a class these men are especially gifted. But the methods by which they have been selected leave much to be desired. They have never been subjected to rigid adaptation or intelligence tests nor judged according to high competitive standards so as to separate the sheep from the goats.

A skillful and robust leadership for a greatly expanded military force is not built alone by the mechanical promotion of its original unit of officers and the sudden induction of an assorted group of able civilian executives. The intrinsic quality and spirit of

[28] Representative Ross Collins, "Wanted for the American Army," *Reader's Digest*, July 1941.

the old Force, whatever its other limitations, are sure to be watered down by this method.

A strong and functioning armed body is not automatically created but is hammered into shape with relentless driving blows, giving it form, character, and dynamism, as well as that spirit of co-ordinated activity which distinguishes a truly great officers corps. The dead timber must all be pruned away. The over-cautious, the antiquated, the pusillanimous, and the incompetent must give ground to the young, virile, imaginative, and daring.

Douglas MacArthur was a brigadier at the tender age of thirty-eight. George Washington was forty-four when he became chief of the American Army. Ulysses S. Grant was in his early forties when he won his great victories for the North. At the height of his glory Napoleon Bonaparte was just turned forty, and the great Alexander was still a stripling when he had conquered half the world.

The elimination of 30,000 Red Army officers in the purge of 1937 served to promote into positions of power great numbers of young, energetic, unspoiled men. General Baratier, in his report to the French Army, asserted that in addition to two-thirds of the General Staff officers, about half the officers in other ranks were included in the purge. "Almost all of the eighty members of the Council of War were quickly liquidated." [29] If the results of this process are to be judged by a comparison of Russian resistance to that of the French Army with its highly touted officers corps, there is much to be said for the business of

[29] V. G. Krivitski, *In Stalin's Secret Service.*

purges. In a free country this routine can be undertaken by periodical competition in the field as well as on paper. Here the officer can be soundly graded and his physical fitness, his ability to think quickly, the quality of his judgment, his originality, and his capacity for leadership measured under the acid test of field conditions.

We should do away with the granting of commissions based on age, which is only another variant of the seniority role. It is interesting to note that the R.A.F. has chosen its officers largely from among younger men. The average age of a wing commander is thirty, and of a station commander, thirty-five.[30]

An elderly high command is not only prone to excessive caution and complacency, but is inclined to accept what it wants to hear. Information which runs counter to its prejudices is dismissed as unsubstantial, eccentric, or extravagant. There are, of course, exceptions to this. Two of the top generals who led the advance in the war with Soviet Russia were von Rundstedt and von Leeb, aged 66 and 65 respectively—both beyond the statutory retirement limit of the U. S. Army. A useful, alert mind and body are not absolutely the product of years alone. There are some men, like wine of ancient vintage, whose quality of leadership improves with the years, and there should be no arbitrary provision which deprives the nation of their services.

In this country in which technology and industrial organization have hit the highest peak of perfection

[30] The U. S. Army rank equivalent to R.A.F. wing commander is lieutenant colonel; to station commander, full colonel.

ever known, there is a wealth of officer material, energetic, alert, patriotic, willing men, some with the true
capacities for inspired leadership. No part of our military, air, or naval establishment should escape this
renovating process, which should seek to rid our armed
forces not only of dead wood but of inertia and unhealthy routine. An active fighting leadership of the
kind given by MacArthur in the Philippines should
be the intoxicating ideal for which we would reach.
That inspired familiarity between leaders and men
which all but died with the system of mass armies,
would return to electrify the combat forces of our nation. The leaders of our armies should be with their
troops and not tied to some communication center in
the rear, and "if the future casualty lists begin as in
former times by long lists of generals, it may be so
much the better for that comradeship in arms which,
more than decorations and stripes, remains the most
noble jewel in the military crown." [31] What a contrast
in inspirational worth to the bureaucratic, almost
anonymous General Staff are the stirring exploits of
General Doolittle and General Royce leading their
dauntless airmen in the first daring forays over Japan!

The whole question of the relationship between officers and men should be entered into scientifically
and with that spirit which befits a democratic nation.
We will be forced to scrap many of our old notions of
military structure. The industrial revolution has affected the armed forces no less than it has affected
every other portion of our basic economy. Even in

[31] General Charles de Gaulle, *The Army of the Future*, pp. 162-
165.

Nazi Germany deference is paid to the equalitarian-
ism this fact imposes. The old salute has been virtually
abolished. Every soldier salutes every other soldier,
whether they happen to be officers or not. The salute
is now merely a recognition of the uniform and not a
mark of inferior status. In this country, where the remnants of an antiquated military structure still persist,
the ridiculous question can arise in the public prints as
to whether enlisted men should be allowed the privilege of going out with nurses.

Most of their ideas for the scientific selection and
indoctrination of men were stolen by the Germans
from two great French thinkers, Le Bon and de
Gaulle, with much contributed by American writers
such as Harold Lasswell and Leonard Doob. We
should not hesitate to borrow these ideas for our own
use and to improve on them. Our only major consideration should be whether or not they are valuable toward the prosecution of this conflict.

All the questions which relate to the morale factor
in German soldiers are carefully studied—the causes of
panic, of homesickness, of general neurosis. The greatest psychologists in the country analyze methods of
inculcating the fighting spirit. The German officer
himself is instructed to maintain an intimate relationship with his men. He must know each man in his
regiment personally, and must be acquainted with his
problems and family life. The new military leader is
never allowed to ridicule a man before others. At conferences in which both officers and soldiers are present,
a friendly, relaxed atmosphere is striven for. For example, all may sit and smoke if desired. The old Prus-

sian caste system is as dead as the dodo. It was scrapped along with the other weaknesses of the old army.

All of this is scientifically appraised and calculated, to insure complete *voluntary* obedience and fanatic faith in the cause for which the enlisted man fights. This is the so-called selective type of blind obedience as distinguished from unconditional blind obedience. Under the grueling test of wartime conditions it seems to function very well and to have no conspicuous weaknesses.[32]

Our present attitude toward these questions is like that of the Wookey in the play of that name, who stated that "morale is a dirty French word and I'll have none of it." There is a lack of definition in reference to the task before the American soldier. The methods by which we attempt to help him make his adjustments are unconvincing. The things which have made soldiers in the past, the crusading temperament, the longing for adventure and revenge, or the team spirit of invincibility such as urged forward the *Grande Armée*, are missing.

There is a certain laxity in the attitude of the American conscript which under the circumstances is inevitable. He is not mentally prepared for war, nor can he be prepared for it by the puttering methods now employed. These depend entirely on the known loyalty of the American soldier. We forget that these men have been torn from their families, businesses,

[32] An intelligent discussion of these factors may be found in the compendium, *German Psychological Warfare*, and Joseph C. Harsch's *Pattern of Conquest*.

and studies. From the view of applied psychology the violence of this drastic change must be cushioned. Men who have never experienced regimentation and who are the product of backwoods isolationism for example, will need to be aided in making an adjustment to a situation whose full import their minds have never grasped. The mere use of abstract terms such as democracy and freedom will not accomplish this. Only a positive and creative concept, which is implemented by the most scientific and modern technique, will do so.

It is elementary that the soldier must be made to feel that this is a great adventure and that he will receive the best of everything. He should be taught to take and like hardship, and to consider his term of soldiering as a privilege which will mark his name with gallantry for the years to follow. He should also be encouraged to think of his new profession in terms of personal success, for the rewards which success brings, appealing directly to his ambition in addition to his patriotism.

From beginning to end our political leaders, as well as our military commanders, should talk directly to the men in the service, encouraging them, explaining their task, and giving them that sense of assurance of which the invincible will to victory is compounded.

v

If we can fashion our entire nation into one total war-making apparatus from which all superfluous factors have been ruthlessly cut away, we could then bring this struggle to an end within the smallest possible compass of time. Nothing could withstand the crushing weight of our will and of our industrial strength totally applied.

Such a result would be a kindness—even to the enemy. The decisive ferocity of onslaught by which we would claim our triumph would be as nothing compared with the rivers of blood which will run, and mountains of commodities which will be consumed if this war goes on interminably as a slow agony of outrage and corrosion. But to accomplish this result— to get away from our softness and individual self-seeking—is not easy. It requires a strong hand and a hard leadership. It requires an end to the eternal pussy-footing and soft-fingered handling of all problems which relate to this conflict. One of the noblest statements ever uttered and one which inspired the British people out of their fear and lethargy when all seemed lost, was a single sentence by Churchill: "I have nothing to offer but blood, sweat and tears."

These are the things which are psychologically sound and which promote self-mastery, determination, and ultimate triumph. Like a soldier in the field, a nation in war must be toughened up, not pampered. It must be told bluntly that victory will not be easy and that every man, woman, and child must pay for it— not only by the buying of Bonds and the surrender of trivial luxuries, but by long hours of the harshest labor, by sacrifice without pay, and by a love for the common destiny which is as strong and hard as steel.

The American people are beginning to understand this and to realize how short our time really is. The restlessness proceeding from this slowly dawning realization is apparent wherever one turns—in the newspapers, in private discussions, and wherever men speak out. *They want action* and are prepared to make whatever sacrifice it calls for.

If we require an incentive as we gird ourselves for battle, we might keep before our eyes the drawn gray face of that great American artillery officer, Eddie King, marching solemnly down a hot, dusty Bataan road, a white flag clutched in his hands. Or the terrible fate of the European women who fell into the hands of the Japanese with the capitulation of Hongkong. Or of the Nazi occupation of Poland which turned that unhappy state into a huge brothel. We could gaze with benefit at the deliberate plundering of all Europe by the Nazi *uebermenschen*, at the brutality, cruelty, debauchery, and degradation which have followed the trail of the hooked cross wherever its standards have rested.

We cannot risk this dreadful picture assuming reality on our own shores. We must make up our minds to it: there will be no peace until the power of Berlin and Tokio has been utterly annihilated—broken and smashed into bits so that it can never rise again.

This must be the last great war. We must never be compelled again to sacrifice our sons and our possessions on the altar of this Moloch.

This is a resolution which can only be made good by the unremitting singleness of purpose of our Republic. Intelligence, energy, vigilance, sacrifice, and endurance will accomplish it.

If we strike now, placing our last ounce of skill, determination, and resource into that crowning tribute to American combat genius, the invincible Armada of the Air, Hitler must fall and drag with him the island citadels of the Mikado.

On that day, which is certain to come, the lazy circling of olive-painted American wings over the black, smoldering cities of the Nazi Reich and of Nippon will proclaim a final end to the mad and lustful bid for power by these outlaw states.

BIBLIOGRAPHY

The Air Offensive Against Germany: an official British Publication.

Annual Report of the Chamber of Shipping of the United Kingdom (1941).

Arnold, Lieut. Gen. H. H., and Brig. Gen. Ira C. Eaker, *Winged Warfare:* Harper & Brothers, New York, 1941.

Banse, Ewald, *Germany Prepares for War:* Harcourt, Brace & Co., Inc., New York, 1934.

Barrés, Philippe, *Charles de Gaulle:* Doubleday, Doran, Inc., Garden City, New York, 1941.

The Battle of Britain: British Air Ministry Record from August 8 to October 31, 1940: Garden City Publishing Co., Garden City, N. Y.

Benes, Vojta, *The Tragic Fate of Czechoslovakia.*

Bengtson, Nels A., and Willem van Royen, *Fundamentals of Economic Geography:* Prentice-Hall, Inc., New York, 1935.

Bomber Command: Doubleday, Doran & Co., Inc., New York, 1941.

Bywater, H. C., *Sea Power in the Pacific:* Houghton Mifflin Co., New York, 1934.

Chamberlin, William Henry, *Japan Over Asia:* Little Brown & Company, Boston, 1941.

Crow, Carl (edited with an Introduction by), *Japan's Dream of World Empire—The Tanaka Memorial:* Harper & Brothers, New York, 1942.

Davis, Tenney L., Ph.D., *Chemistry of Powder and Explosives:* J. Wiley & Sons, Inc., New York, 1941.

De Gaulle, General Charles, *The Army of the Future:* J. B. Lippincott Company, Philadelphia, 1941.

De Haas, J. Anton, *Our Allies, The Netherlands East Indies:* Oxford University Press, New York, January 1942.

De Seversky, Major Alexander P., *Victory Through Airpower:* Simon and Schuster, Inc., New York, 1942.

Deuel, Wallace R., *People Under Hitler:* Harcourt, Brace & Co., New York, 1942.

The Economic Survey of the American Merchant Marine: United States Maritime Commission, November 19, 1937: United States Government Printing Office, Washington, 1937.

Falls, Captain Cyril, *The Nature of Modern Warfare:* Oxford University Press, New York, 1941.

Farago, Ladislas, *The Axis Grand Strategy:* Farrar & Rinehart, Inc., New York, 1942.

Fernandez-Artucio, Hugo, *The Nazi Underground in South America:* Farrar & Rinehart, Inc., New York, 1942.

Fishman, Y. M., Chief of Military Chemical Administration, *Military Chemistry* (Guide for the Commanding Personnel of the Red Army).

Fuller, General J. F. C., *The Army in My Time:* Rich and Cowan, Ltd., London, 1935-36; Ryerson Press, Toronto, Canada, 1936.

Garnett, David, *War in the Air* (September 1939-May 1941): Doubleday, Doran & Co., Inc., Garden City, New York, 1941.

Garsia, Lieutenant Colonel Clive, *Planning the War:* Penguin Books Ltd.

Gayn, Mark, *The Fight for the Pacific:* William Morrow & Company, New York, 1941.

Geil, William Edgar, *The Great Wall of China:* Sturgis & Walton Co., New York, 1909.

German Psychological Warfare, edited by Ladislas Farago: Committee for National Morale, New York, 1941.

Grant, Ulysses S., *Personal Memoirs of,* Vol. II: C. L. Webster & Co., New York, 1885-86.

Grattan, C. Hartley, *Introducing Australia:* John Day Company, New York, 1942.

Harsch, Joseph C., *Pattern of Conquest:* Doubleday, Doran & Co., Garden City, New York, 1941.

Hart, Captain B. H. Liddell, *Great Captains Unveiled:* Little Brown & Co., Boston, 1928.

Herring, Pendleton, *The Impact of War:* Farrar & Rinehart, Inc., New York, 1941.

Hitler, Adolf, and his associates, *Lunacy Becomes Us,* edited by Clara Leiser: Liveright Publishing Corp., New York, 1939.

Report of Cardinal Hlond, Primate of Poland, to Pope Pius XII, November 29, 1939, April 8, 1940.

Japanese War Conduct, A Digest of (compiled by Shuhsi Hsü, Prepared under Auspices of the Council of International Affairs, Chungking): Kelly & Walsh, Ltd., Shanghai, 1939.

Kernan, Thomas, *France on Berlin Time:* J. B. Lippincott Company, Philadelphia, 1941.

Kernan, Lt. Col. W. F., *Defense Will Not Win the War:* Little Brown & Company, Boston, 1942.

Krivitski, V. G., *In Stalin's Secret Service:* Harper & Bros., New York and London, 1939.

Landheer, Dr. Bartholomew, *The Netherlands East Indies Comes of Age:* Netherlands Information Bureau, New York, February 1942.

Lea, Homer, *The Valor of Ignorance:* Harper & Bros., New York, 1909.

Le Bon, Gustave, *The Crowd:* The Macmillan Company, New York, 1938.

Levy, Bert, *Guerrilla Warfare:* Penguin Books, Ltd.

Lewis, Brackett, *Democracy in Czechoslovakia:* American Friends of Czechoslovakia, New York, 1941.

Ley, Willy, *Bombs and Bombing:* Modern Age Books, New York, 1941.

Liepmann, Heinz, *Poison in the Air:* J. B. Lippincott Company, Philadelphia, 1937 (Translated from the German by Eden and Cedar Paul).

Ludendorff, Erich, *Der Totale Krieg* (The Total War): München, Ludendorffs verlag, g. m. b. h., 1936.

Mahan, Admiral A. T., *The Influence of Sea Power Upon History:* Little Brown & Co., Boston, 1890.

Marshall, S. L. A., *Armies on Wheels:* William Morrow & Co., New York, 1941.

Marshall, S. L. A., *Blitzkrieg: Its History, Strategy, Economics, and the Challenge to America:* William Morrow & Co., New York, 1940.

Masefield, John, *The Nine Days Wonder* (The Operation Dynamo): W. Heinemann, Ltd., London, 1941.

Mayers, Colin, *Submarines, Admirals, and Navies:* Associated Publications, Los Angeles, 1940.

Mitchell, Brig. Gen. William A., *Outlines of the World's Military History:* Military Service Publishing Co., Harrisburg, Pa., 1940.

Mitchell, General William L., in a Hearing before a Selective Committee of Inquiry, House of Representatives, Sixty-eighth Congress.

Mitchell, General William L., Testimony of, Joint Committee to Investigate Dirigible Disasters, Seventy-third Congress, First Session, June 1, 1933.

Munson, Gorham, *Twelve Decisive Battles of the Mind:* The Greystone Press, New York, 1941.

Narracott, A. H., *How the R.A.F. Works:* Frederick Muller Ltd., London, 1941.

Pemberton-Billing, Noel, *Defense Against the Night Bomber:* Robert Hale, Ltd., London, 1941.

Rauschning, Hermann, *The Redemption of Democracy:* The Alliance Book Corporation, New York, 1941.

Rauschning, Hermann, *The Voice of Destruction:* G. P. Putnam's Sons., New York, 1940.

Reveille, Thomas, *The Spoil of Europe:* W. W. Norton & Co., New York, 1941.

Riess, Curt, *Total Espionage:* G. P. Putnam's Sons, New York, 1941.

Rosinski, Dr. Herbert, *The German Army:* Harcourt, Brace & Co., New York, 1940.

Raush, A., *Mineral Industry:* McGraw-Hill, New York, 1940.

Sandburg, Carl, *Abraham Lincoln: The War Years*, Vol. I: Harcourt, Brace & Co., New York, 1939.

Schumpeter, E. B. (Editor), *The Industrialization of Japan and Manchukuo, 1930-40:* The Macmillan Company, New York, 1940.

Science in War: Penguin Books Ltd., 1941.

Sforza, Count Carlo, *The Totalitarian War—and After:* University of Chicago Press, Chicago, 1941.

Sigaud, Louis A., *Douhet and Aerial Warfare:* G. P. Putnam's Sons., New York, 1941.

Sweeney, Walter Campbell, *Military Intelligence, A New Weapon of War:* Frederick A. Stokes & Company, New York, 1924.

Taylor, Edmond, *The Strategy of Terror:* Houghton Mifflin Company, Boston, 1940.

Two Years of German Oppression in Czechoslovakia: Czechoslovak Ministry Foreign Affairs.

Van Paassen, Pierre, *The Time is Now!* The Dial Press, New York, 1941.

Vansittart, Sir Robert, *Black Record: Germans Past and Present:* H. Hamilton, London, 1941.

Von Seeckt, General, *Talks of a Soldier:* Berlin, 1929.

Voskuil, Walter H., *Minerals in Modern Industry:* J. Wiley & Sons, Inc., New York, 1930.

Wachtel, Curt, *Chemical Warfare:* Chemical Publishing Co., Brooklyn, N. Y., 1941.

War Against Waste: Office of Emergency Management.

Westcott, Allan, Ph.D., *Mahan on Naval Warfare* (a selection of the most important writings of Admiral Mahan): Little Brown & Co., Boston, 1941.

Williams, Major Al, *Airpower:* Coward-McCann, Inc., New York, 1940.

Willoughby, Charles Andrew, *Maneuver in War:* Military Service Publishing Co., Harrisburg, Pa., 1939.

Wintringham, Tom, *New Ways of War:* Penguin Books Ltd., 1940.

Ziemmer, Gregor A., *Education for Death:* Oxford University Press, London, New York, 1941.